B
BlackBerry® Apps
FOR
DUMMIES®

by Corey Sandler

Wiley Publishing, Inc.

Brilliant BlackBerry® Apps For Dummies®

Published by
Wiley Publishing, Inc.
111 River Street
Hoboken, NJ 07030-5774
www.wiley.com

Copyright © 2011 by Wiley Publishing, Inc., Indianapolis, Indiana

Published by Wiley Publishing, Inc., Indianapolis, Indiana

Published simultaneously in Canada

For general information on our other products and services, please contact our Customer Care Department within the U.S. at 877-762-2974, outside the U.S. at 317-572-3993, or fax 317-572-4002.

For technical support, please visit www.wiley.com/techsupport.

Wiley also publishes its books in a variety of electronic formats. Some content that appears in print may not be available in electronic books.

Library of Congress Control Number:

ISBN: 978-0-470-90302-5

Manufactured in the United States of America

10 9 8 7 6 5 4 3 2 1

WILEY

About the Author

This is what I do. I write books (more than 160 at last count, and of those, 52 are about computers and technology) and I talk on my cellphone and I travel. Sometimes it feels as if I live on my BlackBerry and my laptop computer. I travel all over the world researching my books (I also write about history, sports, and business) and lecturing and consulting.

It is because of that travel that I have become so attached to the BlackBerry. In the past year alone I have been in Denmark, England, Estonia, Finland, France, Germany, Greece, Ireland, Italy, Latvia, Malta, Monaco, the Netherlands, Norway, Poland, Portugal, Russia, Spain, and Sweden. Also, Canada, various Caribbean islands, Colombia, Costa Rica, Guatemala, Mexico, and Panama.

In every one of those places I have managed to keep in touch with family, friends, and business acquaintances from the palm of my hand.

In fact, the initial discussions that led to this very book began with an exchange of e-mails with Katie Mohr at Wiley Publishing in Indianapolis while I was climbing the 17th century Venetian castle of Palamidi in Nafplion on the Peloponnese peninsula of Greece. If that doesn't impress you just a bit, you don't really appreciate the technological revolution that has reached nearly every corner of the world in just the past decade.

I studied journalism (and took some courses to program a gigantic mainframe computer) at Syracuse University. I began my career as a daily newspaper reporter in Ohio and then New York, moving on to a post as a correspondent for The Associated Press. I wrote my first book about computers in 1983 and haven't come close to stopping.

When I'm not on the road and living on my smartphone and computer, I'm at home on Nantucket island thirty miles out to sea off the coast of Massachusetts. I share my life with my wife Janice (who has her own BlackBerry); my two grown children have their own careers and their own phones elsewhere on the continent.

You can see my current list of books on my website at www.sandlerbooks.com and send me an e-mail through the links you find there. If I'm not home, I'll have my BlackBerry clipped to my belt and I promise to respond to courteous inquiries as quickly as I can. Spam, on the other hand, will receive the death penalty.

Dedication

This book, like so many of the 160 I've written, is dedicated to my family. To Janice, who has put up with me for more than thirty years and still laughs at most of my jokes. To my children William and Tessa, who have progressed from laptops (in diapers) to careers and lives of their own. I am proud to be father, husband, and personal IT consultant to the clan.

Author's Acknowledgments

This book bears just one name on the cover, but that's only part of the story.

Thanks to the smart and capable crew at Wiley, including Katie Mohr and the rest of the editorial and production staff who turned the taps of my keyboard and the clicks of my BlackBerry into the book you hold in your hand.

Also, my appreciation to long-time publishing collaborator Tonya Cupp, who managed the process with grace and humor.

I also benefited from the unofficial expertise of the BlackBerry aficionados at Crackberry.com, including Kevin Michaluk and Chris Parsons. For a while, I joined them in living and breathing all things BlackBerry; by the time you read this I will have re-expanded my life to consider other things, but I am comforted by the thought that they are still on the case.

Thanks, also, to many of the developers of the apps I write about in this book. I always do my testing and make my appraisals based on what I find as an unidentified customer, but after the first impressions I sometimes have questions and occasionally problems. Companies that are responsive and helpful (and fix the problem) earn a spot in this book. Those that do not help, including a few that do not answer customer inquiries, did not receive my recommendation.

And finally, as always, thanks to you for buying this book. Go forth and customize your BlackBerry with brilliant, incredible, and helpful apps.

Cover Credits

Wiley would like to thank the following developers whose app icons are featured in the image shown on the front cover of this book:

AP
BeReader
Control BBanel
Cortado
Easy Bartender
File Manager Pro
Fixmo
Later Dude
Pandora
SmartSig
Spam Filter
Tether
WorldClock
WorldMate
Repligo Reader
StickyNote
Shazam

Publisher's Acknowledgments

We're proud of this book; please send us your comments at `http://dummies.custhelp.com`. For other comments, please contact our Customer Care Department within the U.S. at 877-762-2974, outside the U.S. at 317-572-3993, or fax 317-572-4002.

Some of the people who helped bring this book to market include the following:

Acquisitions, Editorial, and Media Development

Project Editor: Tonya Maddox Cupp

Sr. Acquisitions Editor: Katie Mohr

Editorial Manager: Jodi Jensen

Media Development Project Manager: Laura Moss-Hollister

Media Development Assistant Project Manager: Jenny Swisher

Media Development Associate Producers: Josh Frank, Marilyn Hummel, Douglas Kuhn, and Shawn Patrick

Editorial Assistant: Amanda Graham

Sr. Editorial Assistant: Cherie Case

Cartoons: Rich Tennant (`www.the5thwave.com`)

Composition Services

Project Coordinator: Patrick Redmond

Layout and Graphics: Carrie A. Cesavice, Joyce Haughey, Erin Zeltner

Special Art: Melissa Smith

Proofreader: Christine Sabooni

Publishing and Editorial for Technology Dummies

 Richard Swadley, Vice President and Executive Group Publisher

 Andy Cummings, Vice President and Publisher

 Mary Bednarek, Executive Acquisitions Director

 Mary C. Corder, Editorial Director

Publishing for Consumer Dummies

 Diane Graves Steele, Vice President and Publisher

Composition Services

 Debbie Stailey, Director of Composition Services

Table of Contents

Introduction

You're no dummy, and neither am I. The tongue-in-cheek title of *For Dummies* used for this book franchise is one of the world's most successful oxymorons, like military intelligence or boneless ribs. You are smart enough to pick up this book because you know there are gaps in your knowledge. The publisher was smart enough to pay me to fill them in.

Together we make a brilliant team.

About This Book

The BlackBerry is the fruit of the first three decades of high-tech integration and miniaturization. A telephone used to occupy a cube about six inches by six inches by six inches, and a cord connected to another box on the wall.

The first personal computers were about the size of a microwave oven and atop them you placed another large box — a clunky video monitor. Then a big keyboard and a mouse sat out front. And the whole shebang, including a separate modem, plugged into the wall. A camera, even the first digital, was a relatively large box. And my first video camera consisted of a shoebox-sized unit connected by a cable to another large box that hung off my shoulder. And today: all of these pieces and more are integrated and miniaturized to fit into a single unit smaller than a deck of playing cards. Actually, it could be even tinier except that we don't want the keyboard to be too little to use or the screen too small to see.

But it's not the box we are gathered here to celebrate. It's what you can do with the BlackBerry: apps (even the name is miniaturized) are applications or programs or software — any of those terms fit — that use the computer circuitry to perform all sorts of amazing feats.

You can communicate by voice or text or video from nearly anywhere in the world to anywhere else. You can keep track of your investments, your business operations, your favorite sports teams, and your family. The camera in your BlackBerry can take a snapshot or shoot a travel video, or it can be a computer scanner that opens the door to the Internet for product research and pricing.

At last count, BlackBerry App World listed about 10,000 apps. The maker of BlackBerry, Research in Motion, runs this official site. Some of those same apps, plus a few thousand others, are available through third-party sites.

Here are some important truths that show how smart you are to have purchased a *For Dummies* book:

- ✔ Almost anyone can publish an app.
- ✔ Some apps are brilliant.
- ✔ Some apps are truly dumb.
- ✔ It would take months to wade through all the apps and find the ones worth installing on your phone.
- ✔ Someone out there is going to point out that the Apple iPhone site has something close to 100,000 apps. For the most part, that means that there are ten times as many worthless and dumb apps for the iPhone.

And so my task was to look at thousands of BlackBerry apps on the official site as well as those of third parties. I made a first cut to eliminate the truly dumb ones, and then a second cut to leave out the very amateur ones and, finally, a third pass to leave behind the ones that were all sizzle and no steak. I was pretty brutal in my assessment. If an app didn't install properly, didn't run properly, or did not play well with others it did not make my list.

And then from those that remained I chose the ones that were, as the title of this book proclaims, "brilliant." As in shining brightly, outstanding, and highly intelligent. I looked up those definitions on my BlackBerry.

I devote one chapter to entertainment; the remainder are related to getting things done in our lives. Not that I don't enjoy a clever game or disregard the value of diversion in our busy lives. It's just that there's something about the BlackBerry and its users that is different from devotees of some of the other smartphones out there, including that other one from the computer company named after a nearly ball-shaped generally red fruit. Those of us who use a BlackBerry do so because it helps us be more productive, more knowledgeable, and smarter than the next guy or gal.

There are 120 apps that made it into the colorful pages of this book. I'm not saying that these are the only apps worth considering, or that there are not other apps out there that do the same or similar tasks. What I am saying is this: when I sifted through the list of candidates, these were the apps that shone brightest. Over time, there will be new and improved candidates for my list . . . and yours.

What's Not in This Book

Plenty of apps let you read books or blogs on your BlackBerry's small screen, play games on the train or plane, or exchange short messages with friends, family, and business associates. All these apps work just the way you would expect, and I do not spend much time discussing them in this book.

Many current BlackBerry models include GPS circuitry. This allows your smartphone to know where it is and also to work with mapping and direct-finding tools to help you get to a particular destination. I do cover a number of apps that use the GPS to tell you the location of nearby restaurants, ATMs, and emergency services. And some of the apps also can provide turn-by-turn maps and directions.

One type of app does *not* appear in this edition of the book: full-scale software that turns your BlackBerry into a GPS unit that also makes and receives phone calls. These products are now in the market, but they're not quite fully baked. The BlackBerry screen is a bit too small, the controls are a bit too difficult, and the smartphone's memory capacity is a bit too small to allow quick access to maps anywhere, anytime. I am certain, though, that all of these issues will be solved — probably pretty quickly.

Another product that is not in this book are mobile-optimized Web pages. They may be very helpful and very attractive, but they are not apps. They are merely reduced versions of Internet sites.

How This Book Is Organized

In a way, coming up with any sort of organizing scheme for BlackBerry apps is a bit like herding cats: very few of the chosen ten dozen fit neatly into a single category.

If you think about it, every utility is also intended to improve productivity. So, too, is every communication tool. Apps aimed at helping us travel efficiently are also a communication utility. And finance? Well, productivity makes it possible and necessary. What I'm saying here is that I divided the chosen few apps into chapters to make the book easier to read. The classifications are not exact; a utility might also belong under communications. Travel apps help productivity. There are square pegs in round holes.

The first group of apps in each chapter are given a full review across two or four pages. For those reviews I give my opinion of an app's best and worst features. And then, where appropriate, there are shorter reviews for apps that are smaller in scope but still sparkle. Within each chapter, I've chosen one app that was just a bit more brilliant than the others. That one leads off the section and then the rest march behind. I tell you how to get your hands on the software in the "How to get it" section of each review.

And the final chapter of this book is not about apps at all, but instead about accs, as in accessories. I've chosen a double handful of some of my favorite things that accessorize your BlackBerry because, let's face it, even a magician's box needs some props, tools, and flash.

How to Add BlackBerry Apps

The BlackBerry, in a form close to how we know it today, has been around since 2002. That makes it a smartphone old-timer. Its maker, the Canadian firm Research in Motion, has done a good job in maintaining a reasonable level of compatibility across all of its models. However, you cannot expect an advanced app introduced today to necessarily work properly (or at all) with one of the original devices in the line.

Models

The most important dividing line is the version of the BlackBerry operating system used by the phone. There's a kind of chicken-and-egg issue here: older phones cannot run the newer OSes, and newer apps can only function on the more current OSes.

 In this book, most apps require OS 4.2 or later (a higher number) and a handful will only run on OS 4.5 or later. Click Settings ⇨ Options ⇨ About to find the model number of your phone. A line or two down on the screen, the OS is marked as vX.X.X. And then when you shop for an app, pay attention to its requirements.

As this book goes to press, RIM has introduced OS 6.0 and the first of new models (including the Torch 9800) designed specifically for that system. The owners of some other current models can upgrade the OS in their phone from 5.0 to 6.0; however, be careful about doing that until you are sure that all of your existing apps have also been upgraded to run properly.

The other dividing line is between touch and non-touch screens on BlackBerry devices. Current models of the BlackBerry Storm and BlackBerry Torch use screens that respond to the pressure of a finger or stylus; apps that are designed to use that feature will not work on a standard screen.

Sources

BlackBerry apps are available from three sources:

- ✔ RIM's own BlackBerry App World, at http://appworld.blackberry. com from a desktop computer. You can also download a catalog of apps to your smartphone and browse from there.

- ✔ Third-party app stores including www.crackberry.com and its sister site http://software.crackberry.com, as well as www. handango.com/blackberry. Search for BlackBerry apps in your browser to find other sources.

- ✔ Directly from developers. Some app makers and some services like banks, retailers, and browser developers have their own stores.

Installation

The installation of apps can also vary, depending on the method chosen by the developer. The simplest method is called OTA (Over the Air); you give the source the e-mail address used by your BlackBerry or its phone number for an SMS text message. The distributor then sends a live link to your phone, which you click to start the file transmission.

A more complex method involves the download to the desktop of a personal computer of a folder containing the necessary files to install the app. Connect your BlackBerry to the desktop with a USB cable and then run RIM's BlackBerry Desktop Manager on the PC, selecting the Application Loader feature and navigating to the folder holding the files you want to use.

Prices

About prices: it's kind of like shopping for a car. There's a list price, a sale price, a coupon price, and a combo price. Today. And then tomorrow there are new prices. It would not have been helpful to list an exact price as it was when I downloaded the app; we try to help by publishing a price band. $ indicates $4.99 or less, $$ indicates $5 to $9.99, and $$$ indicates $10 or more. Free is just free.

The lowest price is generally listed with the app's title; sometimes you have the option to upgrade a free app with a paid subscription. That information is detailed in the app's description and in the "How to get it" sections.

And you will also find more than a few "free" apps. Some are truly without strings: an airline or a retailer may want you to run something on your BlackBerry that they hope will generate some sales. Other forms of "free" apps are those offered by developers hoping that you will so love their product that you will decide to upgrade to a more full-featured version or buy a different offering from them.

Deleting

Oh, and one other thing: you can delete an app from your BlackBerry this way:

1. Highlight the app.

2. Click the Menu button.

3. Choose Delete.

But if you think you might ever want to reinstall the app, instead use the BlackBerry Desktop Manager and again choose Application Loader. This time, remove the check mark next to the app you want to take off the smartphone (you can remove as many at once as you'd like) and allow the program to store the files for you on the desktop computer.

Icons Used in This Book

Keep an eye out for these icons throughout the book:

I'll bring your attention to the potential for lost data and for unexpectedly high bills.

Don't forget these things.

This might make using the app a bit easier.

Where to Go from Here

Enough of this introductory information in this informative chapter called "Introduction." Proceed into the book. You are hereby granted permission to read it from cover to cover, or from the middle to the end and back to the beginning. Or you can jump right to a particular chapter and start there.

Oh, and one more thing: just like the BlackBerry, this book is meant to be an interactive experience. I'd like to hear from you. Together we can make the next edition even better. You can send me an e-mail at **brilliantBBapps@sandlerbooks.com**. Tell me about new apps you've found that are worth considering in the next go-round. If you're a developer and think your product is worthy, make sure I know about it. And if I agree (ah, the incredible power that comes with my job) I'll send you a free autographed copy of the next edition of the book.

As the British are so fond of saying when someone does something well, "Brilliant!"

1 Utilities and Security

Top Apps

- Repligo Reader
- Ascendo Data Vault
- BuddyGuard Pro
- ControlBBanel
- File Manager Pro
- Fixmo Tools
- PhoneBAK Anti-theft
- QuickLaunch
- Snapscreen
- What's Running?
- Contacts Cleaner
- CropIt
- Find My Phone
- Human Voice Ringtones
- MileageMeter
- Neelam Scientific Calculator
- Parking Meter
- Quick Convert
- Remote Print
- Signal Strength

Repligo Reader
$$$ US

I just bought a nifty new pocket camera to go along with the almost-as-nifty tiny camera that is part of my BlackBerry Bold 9700 and as company for the huge four-pound digital SLR camera that I carry when I'm on a serious photo safari.

The new camera is marvelous, with specifications that are beyond anything we could have imagined a few years ago. That's the good news. The not-so-good news: the camera did not come with an instruction manual. Instead it was delivered with a CD that included an electronic guide to its functions.

I sat down at my desktop computer and read through the 143 pages of instructions and then I went out into the field to try out the camera and promptly forgot the difference between the white, red, and green indicator lights and whether two beeps meant the subject was in focus and four beeps for a problem or was it the other way around?

If only I could carry the manual around in a tiny but still useable form. And then I found Repligo Reader. It is a nicely designed app that opens and reads PDF (Portable Document Format) files on (let's be honest here) the relatively tiny screen of a BlackBerry device.

After I installed Repligo Reader, I connected my BlackBerry to my personal computer and I used the Mass Storage feature to move a copy of the instruction manual for my new little camera (and for my older, larger camera) onto the 2GB media card in my phone.

 These are not small files: one was about 5MB and the other 14MB in size. That's why you need to store them on the removable media card and not in the memory of the phone itself, which is more appropriately devoted to holding apps, contacts, and e-mails.

I could have brought the PDF files to my BlackBerry other ways: send them as attachments to e-mails or download them to the device from the Web site of the camera manufacturer; both of those methods would work but would have been considerably slower.

Once everything was in its proper place, I opened Repligo and I was ready to read to use these manuals anywhere my BlackBerry and I traveled.

There is nothing to configure on the Repligo app itself. Just help it find a file stored on your BlackBerry and tell it to open it for display. Once it is open, though, you can choose how best to view it.

The Whole Page image delivers just what it promises: an entire page of the document sized to fit on the BlackBerry screen. It's a good way to quickly thumb through a manual but not the best way to read it. You can, though, go to the menu and zoom in on the whole page view to examine a section.

But for me, the best feature is the Reading View, which doesn't attempt to hold on to the predefined design of the PDF document and instead renders it in a single column of text and graphics. In this mode I was able to go through the manual as if I were reading it in from a book. (Actually the type was a tiny bit larger and the backlit screen a bit brighter than the printed page.)

Focus	When the subject is focused	When the subject is not focused
Focus indication	On	Blinks
AF area	White→Green	White→Red
Sound[*2]	Beeps 2 times	Beeps 4 times

Another press of the BlackBerry menu key gives you the option of using bookmarks. These are essentially chapter titles created by the original author of the document; you can expand most bookmarks to subsections by clicking the + mark. And finally, you can jump to a particular bookmark by highlighting and clicking it. You can also search for a specific term in the Find utility.

The app includes intelligent page caching, which keeps copies of recently viewed pages in memory and looks a bit ahead of where you are, which allows for faster navigation through large files. And Repligo Reader also claims to be the only native PDF solution that allows you to search for text within documents — a very useful tool.

Other features include the ability to send a stored PDF as an attachment in a new e-mail. It allows you to open RC4- and Advanced Encryption Standard (AES)-encrypted PDF files and attachments, prompting for the proper password when necessary.

On BlackBerry devices using OS 4.5, generally including all current models, Repligo integrates with the e-mail application. That integration lets you use the Open Attachment function to read a PDF file or the Download Attachment feature to store a file on your device.

And using the app with a file downloaded or stored on your BlackBerry does not require the use of any data. You can load up your phone with PDF files and examine them on an airplane or while roaming anywhere in the world without additional charge.

Best features

The difference between using the built-in PDF reader in the BlackBerry operating system and using Repligo is sort of like the difference between looking at a page of tiny print through a straw or through a magnifying glass; Repligo is the one with the magic magnifier.

Worst features

Not really a worst, but the more complex the document the more time it takes to render it for view. We're talking seconds, though, not minutes.

How to get it

Available from BlackBerry App World and from third-party sites such as Crackberry. Cerience Corporation. www.cerience.com. Price: $14.99.

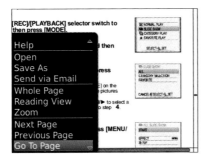

Ascendo DataVault
$$$ US

Every time I travel my wallet comes with me, which is necessary, I guess. But along with as little cash as necessary, in that wallet are three or four credit cards, as well as health and auto insurance cards. I also carry international phone cards for use in places where voice calls made using my BlackBerry would cause me physical pain, and other important pieces of plastic and paper.

The other thing I carry with me almost everywhere, of course, is my BlackBerry. And that is where Ascendo DataVault has earned a resting place: it is a password-protected vault that sits on your BlackBerry and holds any information you choose to put within.

The standard set of categories includes credit cards, bank accounts, insurance information, logins and passwords, and descriptions and serial numbers for your possessions. But this is a free-form database; it can be adapted easily if you want to use it to store any other sort of data that is important to you.

The key to the vault is the use of the Advanced Encryption Standard (AES), one of the strongest encryption systems available to ordinary people like you and me. Your responsibility as a user is to create (and remember) a password that is complex enough to prevent anyone from guessing it.

If someone finds your BlackBerry and tries to open the DataVault they have ten attempts to try and crack the code; after then they are permanently locked out. (If you forget your password, you can tell DataVault to wipe out all of the data it holds on your phone and allow you to start over again.)

And if you open DataVault and forget to log out, it will do it automatically after a few minutes of inactivity. The program can also generate strong passwords — with options to include levels of complexity — that you can use in setting up logins to online pages.

I mean no disrespect to the BlackBerry, but hardly anyone truly enjoys doing a lot of typing on the tiny berries of the keyboard. That's where Ascendo DataVault really comes through: Ascendo sells a bundle that installs on both your BlackBerry and on the desktop of your PC or Mac.

Using the desktop software, I entered a few dozen important financial and personal data cards. Then I attached my BlackBerry to my PC and launched RIM's Desktop Manager and instructed it to synchronize the two devices. In a few seconds, my BlackBerry contained all of the information I had entered from my computer keyboard — and both were protected by the same complex password.

On the BlackBerry you can display information in Tree view, which is a clickable list organized by category, or List view, which is like a spreadsheet. You can organize items by categories and search for any entry by name.

Best features

You can fill in all of the forms and perform all other customization tasks on your desktop and then transfer them to your BlackBerry.

Worst features

I think ten tries at cracking a password is about five too many. And if you are not paying attention it is possible to unintentionally clear the password and wipe out all data. Both of these issues can be easily fixed by the manufacturer. The entry forms are a bit counterintuitive; the programmer was not looking at a real credit card or a real banking account when putting in the standard data categories.

How to get it

Available from BlackBerry App World and from the developer. Ascendo. www.ascendo-inc.com. Price: $29.99.

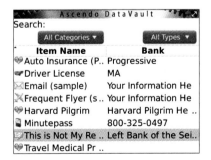

BuddyGuard Pro
$ US

If you lose your BlackBerry, you can hope that some Good Samaritan will find it and give you a call to arrange its return. That's one reason I always have a few obvious listings in my contacts: Home This Phone, Return This Phone, and Whose Phone Is This.

Or someone could take your phone and see what kind of information there is that can be used to their benefit. Or they might choose to remove the SIM card and keep or resell the phone.

One possible remedy is to call your cellphone provider and have service shut off from the phone. That will prevent calls being made on your dime, but it won't safeguard the information stored on the device and it might make it difficult for a well-intentioned person to reach you to arrange a return.

That's where BuddyGuard comes in. It's an electronic bodyguard of sorts, allowing you to use the power of the Internet to take back some control over a lost or stolen BlackBerry. BuddyGuard works by scanning any e-mail or SMS text message sent to your BlackBerry from another phone or from a computer. Some of the commands you can send by e-mail or text message are described here; each command must be followed by the complex password you put in place when you install the app.

bg-alert will play a loud and annoying siren and other sounds on your BlackBerry. If it's still sitting on the table in the airport (or if it has fallen behind the cushions on your couch) it should be found.

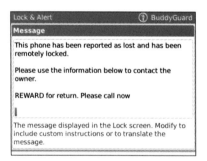

The tone will sound for as long as ten minutes, and will play even if your phone is set to silent or vibrate only. At the same time, this command will also lock your phone and display an information screen that tells the finder how to get in contact with you.

A stranger who finds the phone can silence the alarm with one click and can call or e-mail you from your phone with another. All of the other functions of the phone are disabled. The phone will remain locked — even if it is rebooted — until the proper password is entered.

You can also merely lock the phone by sending **bg-lock**. This command also displays the contact screen.

And there's more: **bg-locate** will use the GPS capabilities of advanced models of the BlackBerry to read the location of your device and send you an e-mail with a link that will open a Web browser to display your phone's location on a map. That's one way to figure out just which coffee shop or hotel room or office you left it in.

Finally, here's the big one: **bg-wipe**. As you've no doubt guessed, this one allows you to remotely and permanently delete data from your BlackBerry. It will wipe out the contents of your calendar, contact list, messages, phone logs, memos, tasks, and any files you have stored in device memory or the media card. In other words, your phone will be locked and unloaded.

Best features

You can even recover your password, as long as you send a request from your own e-mail account using another phone or a computer. The answer will come to where you sent it, but will be deleted on the BlackBerry so that someone else cannot see it and use it.

Worst features

None really, except that the process might be a bit confusing for some phone users. Ask a buddy for help.

How to get it

Available from BlackBerry App World and from third-party sites such as Crackberry. Terra Mobility. www.terramobility.com. Price: $3.99.

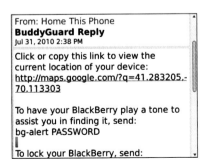

From: Home This Phone
BuddyGuard Reply
Jul 31, 2010 2:38 PM

Click or copy this link to view the current location of your device:
http://maps.google.com/?q=41.283205,-70.113303

To have your BlackBerry play a tone to assist you in finding it, send:
bg-alert PASSWORD

To lock your BlackBerry, send:

ControlBBanel
$ US

The only thing worse than spam on your personal computer is spam in your hand. This simple and useful toolkit allows you to control your BlackBerry apps and consult a banel, I mean a panel, of information about the device.

Under Info, you can quickly learn the following important information:

- ✔ The percentage of charge remaining in the BlackBerry's battery.

- ✔ The unique PIN that identifies your phone and can be used in PIN-to-PIN messaging.

- ✔ The amount of available space for additional apps and the amount of space free on the media card in your phone.

- ✔ The operating system version in use on your BlackBerry.

- ✔ Information about the type of cellular network your phone is using as well as the strength of the signal it's getting.

That's a lot of detail right there in one place. But ControlBBanel goes further.

Click Apps to see a full listing of all the applications loaded on your phone. Press the Menu button on your phone and you can get details about the program including the name of its maker, the amount of memory it occupies, the version installed, and the date you put it on your BlackBerry. And if you are no longer in need of the program, you can delete it with a click.

There's also a panel called R. Apps (meaning Running Apps). This sorts out just those applications that are currently demanding the attention of your BlackBerry. Again, you can ask for details and you can delete the apps if you want.

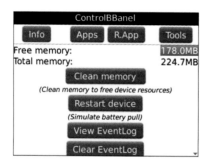

And then under the last tab of this Swiss Army knife of a utility, you have four tools to help you manage your device. If you click Clean Memory, the utility will reorganize the applications running on your BlackBerry to make the most efficient use of system resources. Every time I tried it, ControlBBanel was able to improve efficiency by roughly 10 percent; the more apps you have running on your BlackBerry the more efficient this tool becomes. This is especially so if you leave your phone powered on for days at a time.

The next tool is also very valuable: Restart device. It shuts down the BlackBerry in a controlled manner and then reloads all of its basic software and apps. It's a lot simpler (and less likely to cause wear and tear on your phone) than the traditional hard reboot for a BlackBerry.

If your phone starts to behave oddly or is responding much slower than usual to apps, a restart may be just the thing to do.

The fourth utility on the Tools tab allows you to read and clear your phone's events log. This is serious geek stuff, even for me; it tells you what the phone has been doing all the time you thought it was just sitting there.

Best features

Clean and sober, gives you what you need in a way you want to see it.

Worst features

Not a big nit to pick, but deleting a program within ControlBBanel still requires you to perform a soft reboot of the BlackBerry, just as it would if you deleted it from within the operating system.

How to get it

Available from third-party sites such as Crackberry and the developer. QuiteSimple. www.quite-simple.com. Price: $3.99.

ControlBBanel			
Info	Apps	R.App	Tools

General
Battery:	58 %
PIN:	
Device Model:	9700
File Free:	29.0MB
File Total:	32.0MB
MediaCard Free:	1805.2MB
MediaCard Total:	1881.7MB

Software

File Manager Pro
$ US

The BlackBerry OS is your device's equivalent of Windows for the PC or the Mac OS for Apple computers. With File Manager Pro, the BlackBerry takes one more giant step over the line toward being a full-featured computer in the palm of your hand. This is the equivalent of Windows Explorer on a PC or Finder on a Mac: a full-featured organizer and manager for all of the files stored on your BlackBerry.

You can open up the file structure on the internal (device) memory of your BlackBerry and on the larger media card installed in a removable slot within and copy, move, rename, delete, or send as an e-mail most files. You can create new folders and reorganize the location of documents.

The app can also open and browse a Zip archive (a file or set of files compressed to save space) and you can extract some or all of those files, add to the existing archive, or create a new archive. Just as with a full-sized computer, you can select multiple files and folders to perform the same action on all of them at the same time.

A powerful search function allows you to hunt for files in a single folder or across multiple folders. When you open a folder, you can view the list of files by name or as thumbnails (tiny versions of images from the camera or that you have downloaded or icons representing video and audio material).

If you click a downloaded Word, Excel, PowerPoint, or any file with a native format program, the app will display it using the BlackBerry utility Docs-To-Go (included in current devices running OS 4.5 and higher). If you have a PDF file, it will be opened by the built-in functions of the BlackBerry or by an improved add-in like Repligo (reviewed earlier in this chapter).

You can also use the Text Editor that is part of File Manager Pro to perform more-than-basic editing, search and replace, and other functions. You can also skip several steps by saving files or folders to your Favorites list, which allows you to jump directly to them. And the Favorites are managed dynamically: the ones you use most often (or those used most recently) are moved to the top of the list.

The app permits you to sort files by name, size, type, or date. And you can also examine the properties of any file to learn more details. From that screen you can make a file read-only (meaning that it can't be modified and saved under the same name) or hidden so that it does not appear unless you specifically ask that this type of file be displayed.

Best features

If you know how to use a personal computer, you know how to use this product, and you also know how valuable it can be in managing the files stored in your BlackBerry.

Worst features

Not the fault of File Manager Pro: you cannot delete some of the built-in apps of the BlackBerry and some of its sample files. Although they appear as if they are standalone files they are actually components of the operating system.

How to get it

Available from BlackBerry App World and from third-party sites such as Crackberry. Terra Mobility. www.terramobility.com. Price: $4.99.

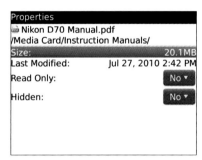

Fixmo Tools
$$$ US

Most of the utilities in Fixmo Tools are ones that I had never imagined I might need, right up until the time when I did.

Here are some of the elements of this BlackBerry tool belt:

✔ **Undelete** is an oops tool. It allows you to retrieve most e-mail, PIN messages, calendar events, contacts, tasks, and memos that you removed from your phone. Now the fine print: you've got to act as quickly as possible to claw back items you have deleted.

The longer you wait the more likely the space the items previously occupied will be written over with new information on your phone or on RIM's servers which sit between you and the people with whom you communicate.

The Undelete tool is available from within Fixmo, and it also insinuates itself into the menu items of your e-mail program. It will also retrieve calendar items, but most likely only from BlackBerry's own calendar and not any third-party add-ons.

✔ **Silencer** integrates with your calendar and completely silences your BlackBerry during time periods when you have meetings scheduled. There's also a Quick Silence button for unscheduled quiet times.

✔ **Forward/Reply with Edit** is a nifty little tool that allows you to easily edit the original message when you reply or forward it. There are other ways to do this same task, but this Fixmo tool is most elegant, integrated right into the existing BlackBerry e-mail menu.

✔ **Flame Retardant** is not a fire extinguisher, but it certainly could pull your ashes from the fire in certain circumstances. It will warn you if you choose to Reply All to a message on which you were BCCed (Blind Carbon Copied); perhaps you just meant to send a response to the original sender.

Other protections in this tool warn against use of naughty words (it won't prevent them, but it will make you stop and think before sending them). Flame Retardant will ask you to stop and think before sending words in ALL CAPS.

✔ **Speed Test** is just what it sounds like; it measures the download and upload speeds of 3G, EDGE, and Wi-Fi networks. It's a good way to find out if slow response is the fault of your phone or the network to which it is connected.

✔ **Battery Watch** expands upon the simple indicator on the screen of your BlackBerry. This Fixmo tool tells you exactly how much voltage is left and translates that into an estimate of how much time for talking, browsing, or other apps. And it also takes your battery's temperature; a very hot battery is not a good thing. You can have it sound an alarm when the power level drops below a certain percentage.

✔ **Memory Monitor** examines your phone's memory use and cleans up the phone's temporary cache to speed up operations. Call Indicator allows you to assign different LED colors for calls, texts, and PIN messages.

Best features

Very professionally designed; head-and-shoulders above kitchen table products.

Worst features

I want these tools on a belt I can wear around my business suit.

How to get it

Available from BlackBerry App World and from third-party sites such as Crackberry. Fixmo Inc. http://fixmo.com. Price: $15.99.

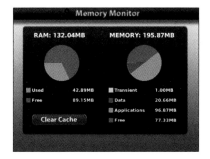

PhoneBAK Anti-theft
$$ US

Here's another take on the shut-it-down, wipe-it-out, and try-to-retrieve-it app. PhoneBAK acts as your agent to report on the approximate location of your phone, alert you if someone inserts an unauthorized SIM card into your BlackBerry, provide details about that usage, and display a warning on your phone declaring that bad things happen to bad people (or whatever else you'd like to say).

It all starts as soon as you download and install PhoneBAK and assign it a killer password; here's a place where you want to pull out all the stops and make it a doozy. (And then please don't write it down on the inside flap of your BlackBerry case. If you need a written copy, be sure to store it far away from where the phone lives.)

This app makes use of the password you set in conjunction with two pieces of identity carried by most BlackBerry devices. First there is the IMSI on the SIM. In something closer to plain English, that is the service-subscriber key (IMSI) that is part of the information encoded on the removable subscriber identity module (SIM) card that is installed in the phone.

Once you configure PhoneBAK on the BlackBerry you can make it sound an alarm if someone removes your SIM and replaces it with their own. The app can also report to you about the new SIM useful information that could be used by a cellphone provider to prevent a stolen or missing phone from accessing their network.

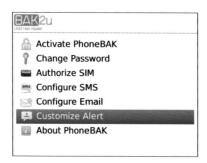

In fact, the message that PhoneBAK sends in this situation would include the phone number being used on the substitute SIM. And it can also report the location of the phone by area code and cell tower ID.

PhoneBAK is automatically turned on each time the BlackBerry is powered up.

Now what if someone doesn't change the SIM but intends to use your phone and troll through the data stored within? That's been dealt with here, too: send an SMS text back to your phone with the command **phonebak+wipe** (include the plus sign) with your very secret password, and your BlackBerry will wipe from memory contacts, e-mails, phone logs, memos, calendar entries, and other information you have preset for the command.

When you set up PhoneBAK on your BlackBerry device, you can enter a list of SMS text addresses and e-mail addresses that will receive alerts from the app if it determines that the phone's SIM card has been changed. You could send a message to another phone you own or to an e-mail account. Make sure any third party knows what you want them to do with this information: in most cases, you'll want them to notify you or directly contact your cellphone provider to inform them of misuse of your phone.

Best features

Another well-thought-out solution to a problem most of us don't want to think about.

Worst features

The onscreen instructions are a bit vague, but there is more help to be found on the developer's Web site.

How to get it

Available from BlackBerry App World and from the developer. BAK2u Mobile Security. www.bak2u.com. Price: $9.99.

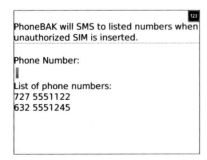

QuickLaunch
$ US

On the one hand, it's great to be able to have a few dozen amazing and entertaining apps stored in the memory of your BlackBerry and ready for use after a few clicks and a bit of navigation. On the other hand, chances are you will use some apps more often than others. That's where QuickLaunch comes in. You can think of it as the BlackBerry equivalent of the taskbar on a PC running Windows or the dock on a Macintosh.

The items you place in QuickLaunch are ones that are available elsewhere, but are more convenient when brought to one place. And QuickLaunch adds a few of its own small but useful utilities.

There is no limit to the number of quick launches or keyboard shortcuts you can set up using this product. To help you keep them organized you can create subfolders that hold groups of apps, using whatever organizational scheme makes sense to you. You can position the pop-up menu on either side of the screen and make it appear within most other applications.

Standard launches include jumps from the home screen directly to a particular Web site, a speed dialer for phone calls, and a shortcut to specific e-mail or text message recipients. And you can also jump to any of the apps that come with the BlackBerry operating system or third-party apps like the ones I write about in this book. You can also jump to a video or sound file to play back immediately; somewhere out there is someone who wants to be able play the "1812 Overture" or "Who Let the Dogs Out?" at a moment's notice.

In addition to putting your favorite apps a pop-up screen away, you can use any of the extra goodies that are part of QuickLaunch. These include a memory optimizer, a utility to clear your call or event logs, and a device reset that substitutes for the battery pull required to restart the BlackBerry for housekeeping or to clear up certain errors.

Other utilities include a mute that turns off the camera shutter noise on most but not all BlackBerry devices, a tilt lock that keeps Storm phones from automatically switching screen orientation, and a menu to set a particular backlight level for your screen. (And a related tool that some people really seem to think is a great use for a smartphone: you can turn on the video camera light to make your BlackBerry into the highest-tech flashlight in the house.)

Best features

QuickLaunch does not run in the background which means it does not use resources until you need it; it runs only when opened. Click on a menu item you've added or enter the keyboard shortcut you have defined, and the program exits the scene until you run it again.

Worst features

There is close to nothing in the way of help for new users. You'll have to figure out how to use the app by yourself, with a few hints drawn from FAQs posted on the Web site for the product.

How to get it

Available from BlackBerry App World and from third-party sites such as Crackberry. Nikkisoft. www.nikkisoft.com. Price: $4.99.

SnapScreen
$ US

One of the first things I had to do when I sat down to write this book was figure out how to capture an image of the screen on my BlackBerry. I could have called in a courtroom artist to make a sketch or I could have used a camera and a closeup lens, but neither of those solutions would have been very satisfactory. Instead, I searched for and found a very capable and reliable BlackBerry app that makes a copy of the image on the screen of my device and then either stores it to the media card or sends it as an e-mail.

Simple testimonial: nearly every screenshot you see in this book was made using this tool. In just a handful of cases the maker of an app had disabled the standard BlackBerry menu display and that made it difficult or impossible to use the utility. I blame that on the other app company, not SnapScreen.

Here's how it works: when you see something you want to copy, press the menu key and then choose SnapScreen. A thin, colored border will appear around the image on the screen. Press the menu key again and choose Send E-mail, select a recipient, and send it. If you prefer, you can keep a copy on your BlackBerry by choosing the Save or Save As option from the menu.

From the options screen you can choose to save images as JPG, PNG, or BMP. For most users, JPG is the best choice. The size of files created with SnapScreen vary depending on the model of BlackBerry in use. The larger the screen, the larger the file (and the higher the resolution on screen or in print).

Using the BlackBerry Bold 9700, captures of the 480×460 pixel screen files were about 38K in size as a JPG, about 5 inches tall and 6.7 inches wide on a computer screen.

If you plan on doing any editing of the image, the best way to work is to immediately save the JPG as a TIF file, which prevents any further compression of detail. Once you are through with any work in PhotoShop or other digital editors, you can make a final copy in any format you choose.

You might want to use the Save to Media Card if you are roaming and don't want to pay data charges. You can send them as e-mails when you return or you can connect your BlackBerry to a computer using the USB cable and transfer the images that way.

This is a very easy, very efficient way to make a copy of the image you see on the screen of your BlackBerry. You can use the captures in designing instructions for others or to show off the features of your mobile device to others.

The one thing you can't do is violate the app maker's copyright. It's fair use to publish a few images for editorial purposes — a review or a guide — but you will need permission if you want to incorporate an image in a non-editorial product, like an app of your own.

Best features

Simple and foolproof, the image you get is as good as what you see on the screen of your BlackBerry.

Worst features

The product would be even better if it offered an option to save or send an uncompressed TIFF file, even though this would be considerably larger than the JPG format.

How to get it

Available from BlackBerry App World and from third-party sites such as Crackberry. Virtual Views Mobile Software. www.virtualviews.com. Price: $4.99.

What's Running
$ US

When cellphones became smartphones — with Research in Motion's BlackBerry helping to lead the charge — they took the next step and became tiny computers. Depending on what I am doing and where I am traveling, my BlackBerry can have 50 or more little apps. Some of them are demanding the attention of the microprocessor in the phone all the time — applications that manage the connection to the nearest cellphone tower or Wi-Fi system, for example. Others only reach out when you ask them to do something: check a stock price, find a restaurant, tell you where you are.

This is all good stuff, but there is a problem lurking in the background: even a super brain like the tiny one in your BlackBerry can become overloaded with too many things to do at the same time. And there is only a specific amount of random access memory (RAM) available to the device in which to do its thinking.

Three things can happen: you can eventually pack so many applications into your phone that there is no room for new ones; you can have so many apps running at the same time that everything will slow down to a crawl, or your phone just might decide, "I've had enough. I'm going to freeze right now and stop working. . . ."

Hooray, then, for the simple but highly informative What's Running app. In two words, it tells you what's running.

Without even opening it (if you have enabled automatic update) the app will show you the total number of apps running and waiting in working memory (RAM). Once you open it, you will see a full list of running apps along with important details such as whether they will automatically be loaded every time you turn on the phone.

```
What's Running (v1.1.1)
(Options in menu)
38 apps currently running/waiting (12% of
295 apps on phone)
        I   Dictionary.com
  A     I   SnapScreen
  A  S  I   Visual Voice Mail
  A  S      net_rim_plazmic_themereader
  A  S      Wireless Software Update
  A  S     |Clock
  A  S  I   Home Screen
  A  S      net_rim_bb_timeddialogapp
  A  S      net_rim_bb_browser_push
```

Is your BlackBerry still running an app you thought you had deleted? (Sometimes free trials of apps will linger long after you have decided not to pay for a license.) With the click of your action key you can take it away. Is an app you want to run refusing to cooperate? From What's Running you can attempt to force it to start without having to go to the bother of restarting your phone.

Users have reported detecting apps that they were sure they had uninstalled, but that remained invisibly loaded and running. Apps and free trials can create hidden apps that stay on the phone after deletion and start automatically every time you reset.

You can also force the deletion of unwanted features of the operating system that are eating up storage space and sometimes demanding the attention of your BlackBerry's processor. These might include foreign language modules and sample images. Be very careful with what you delete here, though; you might want to consult with the customer service department of your cellphone provider or with RIM itself before deleting apps you do not fully understand.

Best features

It does just what its name promises: it tells you what's running — a window into the brain of your BlackBerry.

Worst features

There is no help screen or online support for the product. Your only access to help is to send an e-mail to LSPhone (the developer) and wait for a response.

How to get it

Available from BlackBerry App World and from third-party sites such as Crackberry. LSPhone. Price: $2.99.

Contacts Cleaner
$ US

Do your contacts need cleaning? The solution comes not in a bottle but in a Plug-and-Play app that does what it promises all by itself. With just a bit of regular use, the list of contacts in your Blackberry can quickly begin to look like the clutter on your real desktop: duplicate entries with multiple phone numbers and addresses, partial entries, and other forms of electronic scrap.

Contacts Cleaner is a completely automated process. There are no settings or decisions on your part. Install it and let it hunt down the dupes and take out the trash.

Here's how it works. It begins by identifying duplicate contacts (ones that have the same name for individuals or company name for organizations). One contact is kept and the other one copied into it; duplicate information is discarded.

The product is quick and efficient, and generally does not cause problems, although it can sometimes stumble if you have two or more e-mails listed for the same person. The best way to use this product is to back up your address list to your PC using the Blackberry Device Manager before you let loose the Contacts Cleaner; if there are problems you can always restore the original. Contacts Cleaner will also allow you to restore any deletions it has made if you act immediately after it has done its thing.

How to get it

Available from BlackBerry App World and from third-party sites such as Crackberry. Beaver Creek Consulting Corporation. www. beavercreekconsulting.com. Price: $2.99.

Contacts Cleaner
Stage 1: Find duplicates
Checking:
222
Stage 2: Merge 0 duplicates
Merging:
Stage 3: Save 0 removed duplicates
Contacts Cleaner has finished.

CropIt
$ US

Sometimes it is truly a wonder to find a tool that does just one thing, but does it so well you wonder how you ever lived without it. Such is the case for CropIt, which works with any photos you have taken using your BlackBerry device's built-in camera or any photo you have downloaded to the phone's memory. Use its facilities to locate an image, then set an anchor point in one corner and another in the opposite corner . . . and then crop it.

Why do you need this?

Because almost every photo includes extraneous material, or could benefit from being reshaped. And there is no law that says a picture has to be vertical or horizontal; depending on the model of BlackBerry you use, that's what you'll get. With CropIt you can make a vertical into a horizontal or the other way around, or you can create a square image that may work best as a background for your home screen.

The simple app has just a few customization options. You can choose to retrieve from or to the device memory or the media card, and you can choose to save the altered image as a JPEG or a PNG file. In general I recommend using JPEG, which is a sophisticated, compressed image format that can be read by most other phones and computers. PNG is similar to the GIF format, yielding smaller but less-detailed images than JPEG.

How to get it

Available from third-party sites such as Crackberry and the developer. ALL KAPPS Software. www.allkappssoftware.com. Price: $1.99.

Find My Phone
$ US

My phone sometimes ends up under a stack of papers. My wife's? Well, let's just say we find it in the last place we look (and the last place we'd expect it to be).

Most of the time you can find your phone simply by calling its number. But sometimes it's hidden beneath the sofa cushions. Enter Find My Phone. I like this one because it is very straightforward in setup and it makes a lot of noise and sets off lights — it's like a police cruiser in your living room. The app includes a dozen variations on the alerts it can sound.

The app will override vibrate mode. The only thing Find My Phone (and other similar products) cannot do is set off the alarms if your phone is turned off. (One solution to that: make sure you enable the Auto On/Off feature in Options so that the phone will turn itself on at a time you select; wait until the time arrives and then use Find My Phone to retrieve it.)

The alarm can be triggered by these methods: by calling it three times within 60 seconds (you can allow any caller to do this or set as many as three numbers that are permitted to set off the alarm), or by sending an e-mail or an SMS text message that includes whatever pass phrase you choose. As delivered, you phone will respond to Find My Phone.

How to get it

Available from third-party sites such as Crackberry and the developer. Shao-soft. www.shao-soft.com. Price: $1.99.

Human Voice Ringtones
$$ US

For a short period of time I worked at a prestigious institute at a major university and my secretary had a secretary. Between the two of them, I never had to answer my own phone directly. There was a little speaker on my desk and I'd hear a message: "Mr. Bradbury is on the line." And then I went back to the real world, where I had to answer my own phone.

Somewhere back at the dawn of telecommunications time it was decided to alert phone users of an incoming call by ringing a bell. Then it became an electronic tone, and with the arrival of cellphones many of us chose to use snippets of music.

Now you can get that human touch — in an electronic sort of way — back into your phone. Human Voice Ringtones delivers more than 900 different voice sets for e-mail, text messages, calendar notifications, and just about anything else that would otherwise beep on your phone.

The eight different voice sets include female or male business, cool, regular, or sexy. There are also some funky and mysterious versions. And an equivalent set is also available in French or Spanish. Bonjour señor!

How to get it

Available from BlackBerry App World and from third-party sites such as Crackberry. TeleBEEM. www.telebeem.com. Price: $3.99–$9.99.

MileageMeter
$ US

One quick and easy way to keep an eye on the performance of your car is to look for sudden and unexplained drops in miles per gallon you get in typical driving. Your engine could be experiencing problems, the tires may be underinflated, or your next-door neighbor may be siphoning fuel in the middle of the night.

Which is more likely? You drive up to a gas station with a notebook and pen handy, along with the information about the last half dozen times you filled your car with fuel? Or you arrive at the pumps with your BlackBerry in your pocket or handbag?

MileageMeter is a simple but capable app that accepts basic information each time you add fuel to the tank: the mileage on the odometer, the number of gallons added, the date, and the price per gallon. With that information it produces a report that shows the mpg, the average price per gallon and per mile, and other information (including a prediction of when the next refill will be necessary). To be fully accurate you've got to fill the tank to the top every once in a while; the app takes care of all the internal calculations for partial refills up to that point.

You can keep track of as many as 20 different cars, producing individual reports for each. The reports can be viewed on-screen or sent as an e-mail to your office for more detailed analysis. Or you could send it to your mechanic.

How to get it

Available from BlackBerry App World and from third-party sites such as Crackberry. Thinkomatics. www.thinkomatics.de. Price: $3.99.

Statistics - OneHorseShay
Avg gas consumption: 16.17 MPG
Avg price/gallon: 3.77
Avg price/mile: 0.24
Overall gas cost: 114.38
Best MPG: 19.05 on 8/15/2010
Worst MPG: 12.69 on 8/4/2010
Avg miles per day: 9.3
Most miles with one tank: 240
Avg miles per full tank: 186
Approx. next refill: 141461 miles

Neelam Scientific Calculator
$$ US

Somewhere out there, a BlackBerry owner is asking, "How come I can't do Reverse Polish Notation using the built-in calculator on this so-called smartphone?" And for that matter, why can't we work with sine, cosine, and tangent functions, plus polar input, Cartesian-polar-conversion, and all of the other easy stuff that my desktop scientific calculator can do? Well, that someone out there isn't me. The sort of math I need in my daily life is handled quite well by standard calculators (which use, by the way, infix or Polish Notation for the entry of numbers and formulas). You know, things like 4 + 2 = 6.

But if you're a mathematician, a programmer, an engineer, or just think differently, then the Neelam app just might be the killer app for the BlackBerry. It appears to have this particular slice of the market all to itself.

You can tell this is an app aimed at the inside crowd. There's not even an attempt at an instruction manual or a help screen. It's just assumed that users who need this product will recognize the extra keys on the calculator and know how to use them.

The calculator works with the BlackBerry trackpad or trackball and also with a set of keyboard shortcuts. There are two screens of functions; just press the Shift key and you'll go from advanced math to advanced scientific calculations. Is that cool, or is it not? I have no idea, but I can recognize something that is different, and this qualifies.

How to get it

Available from third-party sites such as Crackberry. Neelam. Price: $5.99.

```
log(sin(3 + 4))

= 0.182443489 A 3.14159265
                          RAD   POLAR

 MC    MR    M+    M-   ( - )      SHIFT    (      )
  1     2     3   DEL    AC          i      ^      √
  4     5     6    ×      ÷          ∠    log₁₀   ln
  7     8     9    +      −         sin    cos    tan
  0     .    EXP  ANS     =         hyp     π      e
```

Parking Meter
$ US

Okay, this one is as simple and to-the-point as you could hope.

You park your car and insert coins (or buy a time card) or simply claim a spot where the sign says something like 30-minute parking. And then you rush around like a mad person to get all of your errands done in time. Or you play it loose and forget about the ticking of the clock. After all, you're made of money; who cares about a $100 parking ticket?

Not me. At least not now that I've got Parking Meter on my BlackBerry.

Choose one of the pre-set time periods or enter a custom amount of time. Parking Meter sets off a really annoying, impossible-to-ignore, and absolutely appropriate siren when time is up. I'd suggest shaving at least enough time to allow you to get back to your car before the meter maid or parking enforcement officer is due to pounce.

Now this product *is* called Parking Meter, and it works quite properly for that very specific purpose. But there is no reason you could not also use it for any other situation where you need to carefully watch the clock: remaining time at an Internet café, baking a soufflé, or running on a treadmill to burn off the calories from the soufflé you ate at the Internet café.

How to get it

Available from BlackBerry App World and from third-party sites such as Crackberry. Didacus Software. www.didacus-software.com. Price: $2.99.

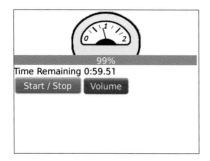

Quick Convert
$$ US

Criminey, it's too hot out there. It's at least 32! You sit there nodding your head as Dundee objects, wishing you could remember the formula to convert Celsius to Fahrenheit. (It's easy: multiply the temperature times ⅘ and add 32. Quickly.) The fact is that we still live in a world where some people use inches and ounces and others millimeters and grams. When I travel outside the United States, I have to remember that 30 degrees is pretty hot, and 40 downright stifling if the place where I am calculates the temperature in Celsius instead of Fahrenheit. And smart as a I think I am, there is no way I can convert from square feet to acres to square meters and on to hectares without the assistance of an app like this one.

Quick Convert is another small tool for special needs: you can convert temperature scales, speed, mass, length, area, and volume. Yes, if the drink recipe calls for two U.S. fluid ounces, a few clicks will tell you to use 147.8 milliliters and not a drop more. And you can speak about hectares with someone who thinks in acres or square feet.

The app is simple and easy to use, although I found at least one minor bug: I entered .5 acre and it came up with a black hole of –2.02 hectares. Once they fix that, or show me how to bend the laws of physics, I'll consider this app a worthy companion for international travel.

The built-in calculator on the BlackBerry is prettier and can do a few conversions, but not as easily.

How to get it

Available from third-party sites such as Crackberry and the developer. Mobilitea. www.mobilitea.com. Price: $5.99.

Quick Convert	123
Type:	Temperature ▾
From:	Celsius ▾
To:	Fahrenheit ▾
Amount: 32	
89.6	

Remote Print
$ US

You've got a wireless phone. Why should you have to use a cable to connect to your desktop PC or to a printer? Well, you don't if you use this utility. It allows you to print or send any file from your BlackBerry (including e-mails, photos, documents, contacts, and just about anything else) using its built-in Wi-Fi.

The app consists of two modules. One installs on the BlackBerry and the other on your Windows-based PC; as this book goes to press there is no equivalent module for Mac machines.

A few important caveats: certain BlackBerry devices, including some models of the Tour and Storm, do not include Wi-Fi. If your phone is Wi-Fi-less, that limits you to use of the BlackBerry Enterprise Server and standard cell data transmission. If your office does not use BES (most individuals do not) this app will not help you. And if you use BES, it might only make sense to employ this app if you have an unlimited data plan.

The app integrates directly into the operating system, using BlackBerry e-mail, address book, and memo applications for quick printing direct from the menu bar.

Setup is a bit complex. You'll need to know some techie details about the Wi-Fi router in your home or office and set some permissions. This may be a job that requires the assistance of the IT department or, for some, a friendly neighborhood nerd.

How to get it

Available from BlackBerry App World and from third-party sites such as Crackberry. Chocolate Chunk Apps. www.chocolatechunkapps.com. Price: $4.99.

```
Connections
─────────────────────────────────────
Add New Connection:
Print server IP address:  (e.g.
"192.168.1.21")
192.168.1.21
─────────────────────────────────────
Print server port: (e.g. "8080")
8080
─────────────────────────────────────
Nickname: (e.g. "home printer")
Sandler Broadcasting Co.
─────────────────────────────────────
Connect via:
⬤ WiFi
○ BES
```

Signal Strength
Free

You may have heard of a computer company named after a large red (not black) fruit and of their misadventures with one of their latest cellphones. According to most experts (except for Apple) if you held it like a normal human being, your hand blocked the path the antenna needed to pick up a strong cell signal. Or perhaps you've suspected that there are certain places in your home or office, or in your neighborhood, where your BlackBerry seems to play dead.

SignalStrength is as simple as simple can be. It displays a continually updating reading of the connection quality your BlackBerry is receiving. Put in on your screen and walk a few feet and see how it changes. Put your hand in any possible position and see if you can replicate Apple's headache; I couldn't find a way to block the connection.

As you use this app, you will have a better understanding of how a structure's design, construction, or contents affect the transmission of radio signals. Large pieces of metal — the sheathing of the exterior of a building or a large filing cabinet or even a refrigerator — may block or distort a signal in a particular spot.

The screen shows the information in two ways: a large version of the five-bar icon (the more green bars the better the signal) along with a numerical reading on the decibel (dB) scale (the closer to zero, the less signal loss, and so a –75 is better than a –98).

Go forth and test.

How to get it
Available from third-party sites such as Crackberry and the developer. Kurlu. http://kurlu.com. Price: Free.

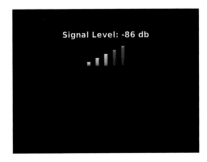

2 Communication and E-mail

Tether
$$$ US

There are more than a few words in English that are considered auto-antonyms: they have at least two meanings that are directly opposite each other. For example, you can cleave something apart or you can cleave unto each other. You bolt the door to keep it closed, or your bolt through an open door to make your escape.

In the world of smartphones, we have another example: to tether a laptop computer to a BlackBerry is to restrain or connect the two devices together. And yet at the same time, a tethered laptop is free and open to the whole World Wide Web. That's the most confusing part about using the BlackBerry app Tether. Everything else is very simple.

Tether (which was born as TetherBerry but changed its name as its Canadian developers began to move beyond BlackBerry and on to other smartphone devices) is a two-piece app that allows your laptop computer to connect to the Internet using your phone's datastream.

Why not just use your BlackBerry on the Internet? First of all, no one would ever say that the experience of using the Web on a smartphone — as wonderful as it is — is as pleasant as a keyboard, mouse, and large screen on a laptop. Secondly, if you need a file or an application that exists on your laptop only, this is a workable and sometimes good solution.

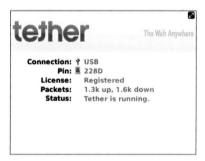

Where would you use such a device? In your home or office you probably have a wired or Wi-Fi connection to a high-speed broadband modem; for most users the incoming connection comes from a cable television or telephone company.

When you're away from home base and traveling with a laptop, you are often dependent upon the availability of a Wi-Fi connection at a café or hotel or office. And there are also times when you find your laptop completely disconnected from the Web — in a car, in the park, in a hotel that wants to charge you $10 an hour for use of their system.

But in each of these places your cellphone probably gets a signal. Today it is increasingly hard to find a place where a BlackBerry cannot communicate. Here's where Tether steps in: a small app on your BlackBerry and a small utility program installed on your PC or Macintosh laptop communicate with each other over a USB cable or a Bluetooth wireless link. When the two devices have fully acknowledged each other, you move your fingers and your attention to the laptop and open its Web browser or its e-mail client and get to work.

In most cases, it's as simple as that. However, here we run into the vagaries of dealing with cellphone providers: Verizon, AT&T, Sprint, T-Mobile, and others. Some are more flexible or more reasonable than others; some are downright ornery.

The first issue: Will the cellphone provider permit tethering using an app they do not sell, own, or control? Most will, but some won't. T-Mobile, for example, doesn't block Tether but doesn't officially support it either; however, if you call in for help, that provider will (surprise) be helpful to its customers.

Second question: Is it necessary to change one particular setting — the APN — on your BlackBerry to use Tether? The Access Point Name is a critical element of the data communication configuration of your smartphone. Some providers deliver their device ready to go with products like Tether. A few require an adjustment to the APN, which is easily done. And a very few flat-out refuse to allow a third party to come through this door.

```
Main screen initialized                    ☑
Connecting via USB
First connection
Trying Carrier Specific APN - MCC: 310
MNC: 260
Registration validation started
Successful (69.60.103.136)
Trying UDP
UDP connection Successful
Checking for USB connection
USB cable is connected to BlackBerry
Tether is Registered.
```

And the third issue, one that is for the majority of users the most important: Will the cellphone provider limit the amount of data you can use per month, or apply a ridiculously high charge over and above your regular fees? Even cellphone providers who offer an "unlimited" data plan may reserve the right to step in if they feel certain users are drinking too much from the common well.

I can't answer these questions for you because there are too many cellphone providers and too many plans available. You can learn a bit about the current state of Tether and the BlackBerry by consulting the Internet and by going to www.tether.com.

It's also worth noting that some phones allow you to have both voice and data connections going at the same time, while others don't. GSM permits both, while CDMA is an either/or proposition. Check with your cellphone provider if you're not sure which type of technology it uses. As this book goes to press, GSM is used by AT&T and T-Mobile as well as many European providers; CDMA is used by Sprint and Verizon and many smaller companies.

Using Tether (or one of a few less-polished but similar competitors) is a bit like playing an extended version of good news—bad news.

The good news: you can use your laptop in places where there is not a wired or Wi-Fi connection available. The bad news: the speed of connection through your BlackBerry will usually be about one-third or a quarter as fast as your direct connection, typically between 1 and 2 Mbps.

The good news: using your BlackBerry as a link to the Internet is generally more secure than using a public Wi-Fi service. You may never need it if someone is listening in on your Internet session in a public place; the likelihood of tapping into your connection through your smartphone is very remote.

The good news: you don't have to sign up for an extra data plan for your laptop. The bad news: some cellphone providers may charge extra for what they consider excessive data use.

The good news: you can conserve a bit of battery power in your laptop by not using Wi-Fi. The bad news: you will use more of your battery power in your BlackBerry as you connect to the Internet. And if you tether to your laptop using a Bluetooth link, that will use up the BlackBerry battery charge even faster.

Finally, there are all sorts of conditions that could interfere with your full use of this app.

And if your laptop, like most, is set up to automatically download antivirus signatures and updates to the operating system whenever it is connected to the Internet, all of that is going to try and squeeze through the same thin straw between the laptop and the BlackBerry.

You may want to temporarily disable updates before you connect with Tether.

Best features

I do not suggest using Tether as your primary way to connect your laptop to the Internet; there are just too many potential headaches. But in a pinch, it works well enough, and just might save your job, your vacation, or your social life. Each license is valid on one BlackBerry, but you can install and use Tether's PC or MacBook software on as many laptops as you want.

Worst features

Tether is a fine idea. It's the cellphone companies that often get in the way.

How to get it

Available from BlackBerry App World and from third-party sites such as Crackberry. Tether. www.tether.com. Price: $49.95.

Antair Call Screener
$$$ US

"I'm sorry, but Mr. Sandler is not available to take your call right now. I'm connecting you to his voicemail." It's nice to have a personal secretary to screen your calls. Today almost all of us carry our own phones and have to manage unwanted calls, unpleasant calls, or interruptions at the worst possible moment.

Well, Antair Call Screener is not quite that sophisticated and polite, but it does accomplish the same thing: if a caller you have listed on your blacklist to be blocked connects to your phone, you will not be disturbed. They are sent to voicemail. The app can also be set to send any caller not in your contacts list or any caller who hides their identity to the same electronic filing cabinet.

As with the other products from this company, this is a nicely designed and polished app that works simply and logically. You can enter a phone number directly to a whitelist (always allow) or a blacklist (allows divert) or make other settings such as allowing or blocking calls from a specific area code or country code, or blocking private callers or numbers that are not amongst those in your personal contacts list.

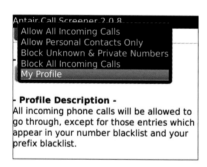

You can add numbers directly to the app, or you can go to the built-in contacts list of the BlackBerry and use the menu key to add numbers there to a whitelist or blacklist. (I maintain a set of "Do not accept" numbers in my contact list — telemarketers and other professional annoyers; I easily added all of them to Call Screener's blacklist.)

You can also set up more than one screening profile and switch between them. For example, you could have a profile that blocks all unknown callers when you are at work. Or you could allow certain callers to get through while you are busy and then change to a different profile to allow anyone not on the blacklist to get through. The app also allows you to easily see the details of all blocked calls, including the ability to call them back with one click.

As an example of the attention to detail of this app, I found that my BlackBerry would ring once before blocked calls were sent to voicemail. That was not the way I wanted it to behave, so I went to the settings screen and adjusted the sensitivity level of the app; after I made the change, unwanted calls were diverted in silence.

The app is available as a free trial so that you can see how it works; after 15 blocked calls it is disabled until you purchase an activation code.

Best features

The ability to have multiple profiles allows you to customize the way the app works depending on where you are and how willing you are to be interrupted.

Worst features

The one other feature I hoped for, a block that simply hangs up on unwanted callers rather than sending them to voicemail, is not included. I would rather that unwanted callers not even know they ever reached my phone. Unfortunately, this is a function that is under the control of your cellphone service provider. Check with them to see if that option can be enabled on your phone; my provider, a company whose name begins with T-, does not yet cooperate in this way.

How to get it

Available from BlackBerry App World and from third-party sites such as Crackberry. Antair. www.antair.com. Price: $49.99.

```
Call Screener Statistics
Performance Information:
Calls Blocked: 3
Calls Allowed Through: 0

Current Profile Information:
Profile: My Profile
Whitelisted Numbers: 0
Blacklisted Numbers: 2
Whitelisted Prefixes: 0
Blacklisted Prefixes: 0
```

Antair Snippets
$$ US

This very attractive and useful utility is one that you should consider including in your basic BlackBerry portfolio.

I like that first sentence. In fact, I think I might use it again in another part of this book. And I might want to insert it into an e-mail or perhaps a text message to people who write me asking for suggestions about BlackBerry apps.

Antair Snippets is an app that creates and stores what programmers used to call "macros." With a click of the BlackBerry Menu button, you can insert a predefined snippet of text to speed your work in e-mails, text messages, Twitter tweets, and just about any other form of electronic communication.

You can also use the app to create a set of different signatures to go at the start or end of e-mails you send; you could have one signature with full personal contact information to send to friends and trusted business contacts, another with minimal information to go to people you don't want phoning you in the middle of the night.

The app comes with a set of a few dozen generic snippets, things like, "Should you require any further information, please do not hesitate to contact me."

You can create snippets from within the app and store them in predefined or custom folders. Or you can create a shortcut from within the BlackBerry e-mail program by clicking the Menu button and choosing Create Snippet.

You can also launch a snippet by entering just a shortcut code, which Antair calls Quick-Type. I created a snippet to send to people who e-mail me with a question while I am traveling; it thanks them for their kind words about my books and promises a more fulsome response when I return to my office. To insert that, I just type away_msg and press the spacebar and all of those words come tumbling out of Snippets and into my e-mail or text message. When you have an e-mail that you think will come in useful in the future, you simply choose Create Snippet from the menu. The app will pick up the text and store it for use later.

There's not much in the way of instructions within the program, although if you visit Antair's Web site you can see an illustrated walk-through and even a short video. And when you register the program, the company sends you an e-mail with helpful quick tips. If you work in sales, for example, you can add a full set of snippets that include product descriptions, shipping policies, and warranty information. And then when you receive an inquiry from a customer you can quickly construct a response using prewritten snippets of text.

On the customer-service side, you could have at the ready a set of instructions for troubleshooting or repairing a product. "You're having some difficulty adjusting the brightness on your video projector, I see. Here are some steps you can try right now that may solve the problem." Select, click, send: bingo.

Best features

This is one of the most professionally designed and attractive apps available for the BlackBerry, and it delivers all it promises.

Worst features

On-screen navigation within the app itself is a bit sloppy using the trackpad on a Bold 9700; there are no such problems invoking the app from within the BlackBerry e-mail program, though.

How to get it

Available from BlackBerry App World and from third-party sites such as Crackberry. Antair. www.antair.com. Price: $9.99.

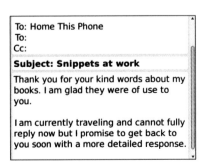

Antair Spam Filter
$$$ US

I've been walking the streets of Paris and have heard the chime from the BlackBerry on my belt: would I like to buy a genuine replica Rolex? No I wouldn't, and I also don't want to be interrupted in a business meeting by an urgent message offering illegal downloads of copyrighted books.

Many BlackBerry users are caught between a rock and a hard place. We very much want to be able to maintain our electronic connection to home and office — that is one of the beauties of the mobile device — but we don't want to be interrupted unnecessarily.

The PC that sits on my desk in my office and the laptop I take with me on trips each use a pretty capable spam filter that diverts known garbage and suspected trash to a separate folder within my e-mail program. I can troll through that collection quickly and rescue the few worthy pieces of communication that slip through. But my BlackBerry connects directly to the company that manages the domains I own. Different rules are in place for e-mail that goes directly to my BlackBerry. And thus, the messages for illicit pharmaceuticals, unwanted advances from unknown people in strange places, and any of a hundred other petty or major annoyances still come through almost anywhere I travel.

That is, until I added Antair Spam Filter to my armamentarium. It insinuates itself into the BlackBerry e-mail application and also integrates with your contacts list and reads all of your incoming mail. It stops junk where it counts — at the BlackBerry.

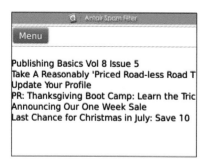

It begins working as soon as you install it, filtering out known junk. You can, if you choose, fine-tune its operation by adding e-mail addresses or entire domains (the part of an address after the @ sign) to either a whitelist or a blacklist. Sources on the whitelist are always considered acceptable; those on the blacklist don't get through. You can also add a list of words and phrases to a whitelist or blacklist.

Antair Spam Filter works with any e-mail delivered to your BlackBerry, both corporate and personal accounts.

When it catches a known or likely suspect, three things happen:

1. The message is removed from the e-mail listing on your BlackBerry.

2. The original message is left on the e-mail server where it will be picked up by whatever e-mail client software you use on your computer (such as Microsoft Outlook or Outlook Express or Apple Mail).

3. The subject line for the suspected spam is moved to the Spam Box that exists within Antair Spam Filter. When you choose to visit the folder you can throw out the garbage, read individual items, or restore any or all of the messages held there. If you restore something from the Spam Box, the sender's address is automatically added to the whitelist.

Best features

The software works silently in the background, removing suspect spam messages as they arrive in your e-mail inbox without even ringing your BlackBerry chime. You'll get a notice to check the Spam Box, and you can do it on your own schedule.

Worst features

Not really a worst, but a fact: the "free trial" is limited in function. It's enough to give you a sense of the app, but you'll need to buy a license for full functionality.

How to get it

Available from BlackBerry App World and from third-party sites such as Crackberry. Antair. www.antair.com. Price: $49.99.

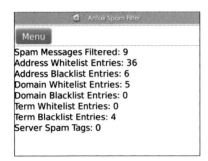

BerryBuzz
$$ US

If you had any doubt about whether there really is a programmable computer beneath the sleek covers of your BlackBerry, this app should resolve them. BerryBuzz performs what programmers call tweaks. Specifically, it tweaks nearly all of the settings of the built-in alert system of the BlackBerry. Never mind that RIM says your phone should blink red for no more than 15 minutes when a new e-mail arrives; if you want to change the operating system so that it glows a fearsome fuchsia or an intimate indigo, and continue to do so until you tell it to stop, well then go forth and tweak.

There's not much that is not adjustable using this tool. You can set separate LED colors for each e-mail account on the phone. The same applies to PIN messages, instant messages from BlackBerry, AOL, Google, Twitter, and Yahoo!, SMS or MMS texts, calendar alerts, tasks, and missed phone calls. And you can program the app to set the custom alert for a growing number of third-party apps.

You can deal with one of the little annoyances of the BlackBerry operating system and insist on receiving both a vibration and a tone at the same time for incoming calls and notifications. Another nifty feature is the ability to instruct your smartphone to vibrate or play a sound when a call is connected or disconnected. And you can back up and restore settings you make with this app to and from the media card.

You can assign specific colors to specific people: hot red for that special someone, threatening orange for the boss, and playful green for your buddies. You can stack two LED colors or use 12 rapid-flashing disco colors to draw attention to your phone. We're only just beginning: you can set the speed of the LED flash. And you can define a schedule for hours of the day or days of the week when all LED flashes, beeps, and vibrations will be muted.

All of this might sound like a great big waste of battery power. They've even thought of that: BerryBuzz is designed to use as little power as possible, and you can also set it to slow down or stop to save power if you're away from the phone or otherwise choose to ignore its insistent beckoning.

One potential issue with using a product like BerryBuzz is that you may end up with a BlackBerry device that is so customized to your personal preferences that it will look and perform very differently from all of the others of its type. (Like I say, that may or may not be a problem — I don't like others playing around with my device.)

More significantly, if you change some of the ways the BlackBerry works, you may have difficulty obtaining technical assistance because the experts trying to help you will be working with a standard group of settings. The solution is to fully understand and keep track of any changes you make so that they can be undone or worked around in the event of a problem.

Best features

You've got to respect the developers of this app for coming up with a list of just about every possible modification for the notification system. The only thing missing is a feature that has your BlackBerry stand up on its end, do a twirl, and finish with a yodel.

Worst features

There's not much in the way of instructions or help screen; you'll have to spend some time playing with the settings to learn how to use them and see whether they meet your needs. Then again, for a certain group of people, tweaking the operating system is fun in and by itself.

How to get it

Available from third-party sites such as Crackberry. Bellshare. www.bellshare.com/berrybuzz. Price: $5.95.

Call Blocker Pro
$$ US

The good news about having a cellphone — especially a highly advanced smartphone like the BlackBerry — is that anyone can reach you just about anywhere.

That's also the bad news.

Like it or not, telemarketers and political action committees and old flames can reach out and annoy you at a click of a button. It doesn't help all that much if you (as I do) attempt to keep your cellphone number out of directories and don't list it on forms or on Web sites.

The fact is that unless you go out of your way to block the display of your phone number, any time you call someone from your BlackBerry or any other brand of cellphone, that number will be captured by the person you call. Just take a look at the recent call listing on your own device.

Call Blocker Pro is like having an answering service for your BlackBerry. You can instruct it to block a specific phone number, an entire area code, or any call from someone who is not listed in your contacts. You can also block calls from anyone who hides their own phone number with a caller ID that reads Private Call.

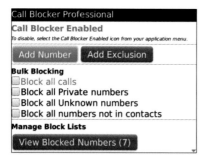

You can create exceptions — a whitelist — to allow certain numbers to get through no matter what other conditions you set. Other options allow you to specify exactly how the calls are handled. One selection sends all blocked calls directly to your voicemail. That allows you to pick and choose how you want to handle calls; however, it also lets the caller know that you exist and they may be able to learn some details from whatever is in your answer message.

The other option is "pick up and hang up" which is just what it sounds like: the caller hears only a click, and doesn't know if the number is still valid or learn anything else about you.

The app includes a timer mode that allows you to turn on and off the blocker at particular times. You could use this to ensure that only people who are in your contacts list can call you during business hours or only when you're not at work.

And, if you choose, you can also instruct the app to send an SMS text message to all blocked callers. It might say, "Sorry, I can't take your call right now but I'll listen to your voicemail and get back to you soon." Or you could choose this sort of message: "I'm not going to take your call. Not now or ever. So stop trying."

Best features

Attractively and thoughtfully designed, it is very easy to set up and use.

Worst features

It's not a worst feature, but there are a few caveats: annoying callers are constantly looking for ways to bust through call blocking programs. They could change their number, or they could try to defeat blockers.

How to get it

Available from BlackBerry App World and from third-party sites such as Crackberry. Epic Applications. www.epicapplications.com. Price: $2.99–$5.99.

Caller ID Reader
$$$ US

When someone calls me at my office on my wired phone (actually, it uses the local cable television company's fiber optic connection) I wait a beat before picking up the handset to allow the device to announce the name of the caller.

It's the closest I come these days to having a secretary screen my calls. Does anyone still have an arrangement like that?

Until very recently, though, if a call came in on my BlackBerry I would have to glance at the screen to read the name of the caller; that was half of an electronic loaf.

Now, with the addition of Caller ID Reader, I have my whole loaf and I can hear it, too: the name of most callers is now announced on my BlackBerry with each incoming call.

Caller ID Reader comes from the same company that makes the DriveSafe.ly app that reads aloud incoming e-mail and text messages, and it uses the same very clear and easy to understand computer-generated voice to announce callers.

The app comes in a free version with incoming caller names from your address book. The first time a call is received, the app will announce the incoming phone number; after the phone call is over, the app will look for the caller's name in your contacts list.

The free version is free but only up to a point; after every third use your phone will somewhat indignantly suggest that you upgrade to the paid version. You can ignore that message and get three more freebies each time. Or upgrade to Pro for commercial-free use.

Caller ID Reader™ Ver. 3.3
You Must Set Your Phone Sound Profile to Vibrate or Silent.
Caller ID Reader™   On

Audio Output: Speaker ▾
Volume: 90
☑ Override Slient Mode
Account
Purchase   Account Info

Advanced   ▾

The app is also compatible with most Bluetooth wireless headsets and with radio rebroadcasters that send incoming phone calls to your car radio.

As with DriveSafe.ly, this product connects to your Internet to convert text to audio and therefore is using your data plan. I would suggest you be very wary if you do not have an unlimited data plan or if you use your phone while roaming internationally.

One other point: if the caller chooses to hide his or her name or phone number, all you will hear is "Private Number" or sometimes a bit of gibberish. Unfortunately, there's not anything you can do about callers who choose to hide their identity.

Some are people who feel it necessary to do so for privacy reasons including some health care providers. Some are annoying telemarketers. And some just don't want you to know who they are before you answer the phone. You can always press the red button on your BlackBerry and ignore the call.

For the rest, though, Caller ID Reader gives us a fighting chance.

Best features

It works well, delivering a name or number of an incoming call whenever possible.

Worst features

The "free" version is actually closer to a trial version, inserting a message asking you to upgrade after every third caller. If you find the feature useful, the Pro version is the way to go. It is available on a monthly subscription or an annual package, with one rate for personal use and another for business use.

How to get it

Available from BlackBerry App World and from third-party sites such as Crackberry. iSpeech.org. www.calleridreader.com. Price: $9.95–$19.95.

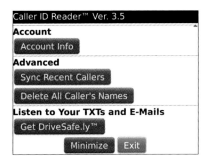

DriveSafe.ly
$$$ US

Add to the list of hazards on the highway (loud music, putting on makeup, and talking on a cellphone) a particularly pernicious problem: texting while driving. It's ridiculous to claim that reading words on your BlackBerry (or even worse, sending an e-mail or a text message while driving) is a rational thing to do. It takes your mind and your eyes off the road and at least one hand off the wheel. 'Nuff said? But lots of people do it, and many states — several dozen as this book goes to press — have passed laws against it. It still happens, though.

That's the reasoning behind the oddly named DriveSafe.ly mobile app. At the BlackBerry end of the electronic connection, it is a very advanced text-to-speech system that intercepts incoming SMS text messages and e-mails and reads them aloud to you. The free version of DriveSafe.ly will announce the first 25 words; the paid versions can read as many as 500 words of your message. Depending on the settings you choose, the very clear and real-sounding reader can tell you the name of the sender, the subject, and some or all of the message.

The app is simplicity itself in installation; it integrates with the e-mail and text message configuration of your phone. All you have to do is turn it on; you can set it to automatically load anytime the phone is booted or you can turn it on or off so that it is available only when you need it.

DriveSafe.ly will also integrate with any special arrangements you have made on your phone for hands-free use: Bluetooth headsets or transmitters that replay your cellphone through your car radio, for example.

And there is one other option that can be very valuable for some users. You can choose to have DriveSafe.ly automatically respond to every incoming text or e-mail with a message of your choosing.

For example, you can instruct the app to respond to all senders like this: "Thank you for your message. I am driving right now and cannot immediately respond, but I will get back to you as soon as possible." At first, I thought this was a great idea. Now, I'm not quite so sure. The auto-respond feature does not distinguish between friends and foes. Any spammer whose message gets through will also get a note from you.

In general, I recommend that computer and BlackBerry users do not respond in any way to spam. Don't attempt to unsubscribe or send back a threat. All you are doing is confirming that the e-mail used by the spammer is an active one; it's pretty likely this will move your address higher up on the list for future electronic junk mail.

The electronic voice used in the program is among the best I have heard. It uses the sophisticated technology of iSpeech, a company that is very active in converting Web pages, documents, and messages to voice.

The downside to this very sophisticated text-to-speech conversion is that the work takes place on a computer somewhere else. Leaving aside the fact that this means that your private e-mails are being electronically diverted over the Internet to somewhere else, it also means that your BlackBerry is using your data plan in both directions.

Best features

Very smooth text-to-speech conversion and nicely designed and polished app.

Worst features

I would not recommend using this app unless you have an unlimited data plan or can afford to pay for data usage without limit.

How to get it

Available from third-party sites such as Crackberry and the developer. iSpeech.org. www.drivesafe.ly. Price: Free for basic version. Pro upgrade $15.

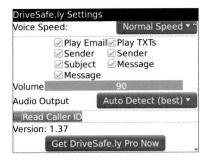

SmartSig
$ US

The sig is that little snippet of text that goes after your e-mail message. Sig, as in signature. It's the computer equivalent of the information on a business letterhead; somebody out there must still send letters on stationery, I imagine.

This simple app allows you to create a whole bunch of different sigs — for different purposes or to customize the response from multiple e-mail accounts you may have set up to funnel into and out of your BlackBerry. SmartSig works well, and pretty much exactly as you would expect. You begin by giving a name to a sig and assigning it to an e-mail address.

You can use any of the letters, numbers, and characters available from the BlackBerry keyboard. (No boldface or italics or special fonts, at least from within this particular utility; you may need to find another app for that purpose.) And then you save it to the memory of your device and create a few more.

The next step is to enable or disable the sigs you want to apply. If you have only one sig for each of several e-mail accounts that are used by your BlackBerry, you can enable them all and the app will select the proper one to go with the outgoing message.

On the other hand, say you have created a personal and a business sig for the same e-mail account. You need to enable one or the other before sending mail. It takes another step but you can do that by clicking the menu key from within the e-mail utility of your device and choosing SmartSig; that takes you right to the display of available signatures and you can enable or disable them as you need.

This app adds one other function that is not ordinarily part of the BlackBerry toolkit: it applies the same (or if you prefer, different) sigs to outgoing SMS text messages.

One irritation that is not the fault of SmartSig: this app does not remove the "sent from my BlackBerry" line added by your cellular service provider. To get rid of that you'll have to edit the BlackBerry Internet Service settings. Consult your cellphone company for assistance if you need it, and don't take "No" for an answer. With this utility on your smartphone you really do not need to carry free advertising for your cellphone provider.

Best features

One of the beauties of the BlackBerry is how it fits so nicely with both business and personal communication and smartphone functions. SmartSig extends that just a bit to make your e-mail and SMS messages appropriately professional or nicely casual as needed.

Worst features

It would be nice to have a click-and-apply menu of all of the sigs you have defined so that you could quickly choose one to match the message you are sending. Even better would be something like this: the ability to embed a keyword in a message and let SmartSig figure out which sig to attach.

How to get it

Available from third-party sites such as Crackberry and the developer. Swift Raven Software. www.swiftraven.com. Price: $1.50.

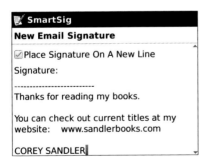

WhereRYu?

$$$ US

It used to be so much easier to get lost before the days of cellphones and then GPS units. And with current models of the BlackBerry incorporating a GPS, you can ask an app to tell you exactly where you are. And so it was just a relatively minor leap forward for a programmer to figure out a way to allow a trusted someone else to ask your BlackBerry to report in on command.

Here's how it works: you download and install WhereRYu? on your own BlackBerry . . . or on your child's smart device. From the phone you add at least one trusted e-mail address. And then you send an e-mail from a trusted address to an e-mail account monitored on the BlackBerry. In the subject line, place WhereRYu? (or if you prefer real English words, Where Are You?).

All by itself it will check its location using GPS and reply to the e-mail with a message that says, "I am here" and supply a link to a Google Map. The e-mail can be read on another smartphone or on a desktop computer — any device that has access to one of the trusted e-mail addresses. If all goes well, the GPS report will place the location of the phone very precisely.

Now there are some caveats:

- ✔ The phone has to be turned on.
- ✔ The user has to allow you to place the app on the phone and enable its access to the GPS chip.
- ✔ The BlackBerry has to have good communication with a few of the GPS satellites overhead. The current version also has limited ability to determine its location based on the identity of the nearest cellphone tower.

The maker of the app advises that you can choose to hide an app from display in the downloads folder. However, the user will still see an incoming e-mail and an outgoing response.

Some phones, including many CDMA models from Verizon, do not ordinarily have their GPS chip enabled. Check with your provider or the maker of this app if you are unsure about whether your BlackBerry will work with this tool.

So this product is not quite a super-secret spying device that lets you check up on someone else without their knowledge. On the other hand, it might offer some reassurance to parents if both sides agree to use this simple app. And although it is not the primary purpose of this app, you can also use it to find your phone if you have misplaced it somewhere. It's not going to tell you if it is in the sock drawer or the kitchen cabinet, but it should tell you if you left it at work or in the supermarket.

Best features
It offers a bit of reassurance in these complex times.

Worst features
The user of the BlackBerry has to cooperate on several levels. If the phone is switched off, the app is removed or disabled, or the list of trusted e-mails is cleared or edited you won't get an answer to your WhereRYu?

How to get it
Available from BlackBerry App World and from third-party sites such as Crackberry. Volcari Software. www.volcari.com. Price: $39.99.

From: Home This Phone
Re: WhereRYu?
Aug 5, 2010 8:32 AM

I am here:
http://maps.google.com/
maps?q=41.27339%2C-70.113096

Static map (better suited for mobile devices):
http://maps.google.com/
staticmap?markers=41.27339,-
70.113096&size=320x240&zoom=10&k

Antair Auto-Responder
$$$ US

This is the e-mail complement to the Antair Call Screener reviewed earlier in this chapter. Antair, if you haven't figured it out by now, has produced an entire line of very capable and professional tools for the mobile professional; they're priced as such, too. So while the call screener is capable of managing the flow of phone calls from specific people or numbers, the Auto-Responder can do the same for some or all of your incoming e-mail.

Do you want everyone sending you mail to know that you are out of the office and will not be able to respond for the next ten days? You can do that. (Although some people will say, "He does have a BlackBerry, doesn't he?") Would you like most of your friends or clients to get a message saying you are in a meeting for the next few hours and can't immediately respond, but send that special someone (your significant other, or your boss, for example) a separate message or none at all?

Antair Auto-Responder allows for creation of global responses that go to all e-mailers and custom responses that are sent only to specific senders. You can use their predefined messages or create your own, and you can tell the system how to respond if one particular sender keeps trying to get through — it might be important, or it might be spam, but you might want to know. Once you have your responses set up, you can turn them on or off very quickly.

How to get it

Available through BlackBerry App World and third-party sources like Crackberry or from the developer. Antair. www.antair.com/blackberry/autoresponder. Price: $49.99.

Antair Headers
Free

Here is a tiny (19K) app at a great price (free) that gives you just a bit of extra information that may help you analyze the nature of an e-mail and perhaps a bit about its sender. There is no icon for the app; it just inserts itself into your BlackBerry e-mail application.

When you press the Menu key you will find an additional option called View E-Mail Headers. The screen you see generally includes the e-mail address (and sometimes an individual's or company's name) for the sender and tells you which one of your registered e-mail accounts it was sent to.

The header also includes the subject and the date and time the message was sent and then received by your mail server. (Depending on how your phone is set up, this could be the BlackBerry server, your company's own server, or a third party like AOL, Google, or Yahoo!)

As you undoubtedly know, the e-mail system has been deeply corrupted by spammers and other creeps. They have become pretty good at faking the From information and other details in a header. For that reason Antair Headers is not going to always be helpful in spotting suspicious or downright false communication. But this app can serve as your front-line defense in examining a piece of mail. If the message says it's from your Best Friend Forever but the header tells you it's from your Worst Enemy Ever, you'll be all the wiser and safer.

How to get it

Available through BlackBerry App World and third-party sources or from the developer. Antair. www.antair.com/blackberry/headers. Price: Free.

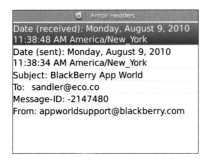

Flag Your Emails
$ US

This app may well win the prize in this very special category: Doing Something Valuable (and One Thing Only) Very Well and For Only a Few Dollars.

Flag Your Emails . . . flags your e-mails . . . with a nice bright red exclamation point. Now you don't want to do this on all your e-mails — that would be defeating the purpose. Instead you put a flag on mail you have received and that is waiting in your inbox as a reminder to hold on to it or to do something about it or to otherwise distinguish that message from all the others that surround it. The concept of flagging comes from the world of computers, where an e-mail program typically allows you to attach symbols to messages to remind you to respond to them quickly or to help you find them easily the next time you troll through the stack of messages.

Now I fully expect that sooner or later Research in Motion will add this function to the operating system for newer models of Blackberry devices. But for the rest of the universe, here's a way to raise a flag.

How to Get It

Available from BlackBerry App World and from third-party sites such as Crackberry. The Jared Company. www.jaredcompany.com. Price: $2.99.

Mail Rule Manager
$ US

If I get another piece of mail offering me cheap Rolex ripoff watches I'm going to turn back the hands of time. And the same goes for messages that come from that "friend" I met at the reunion a few years ago who keeps trying to sell me insurance. A capable anti-spam filter will probably catch the Rolex offer unless the spammer manages to get one step ahead of the defenses (sending images instead of text or spelling R0lex using a zero instead of the letter O).

But diverting a message from a specific person or domain or following a specific set of rules to discern the difference between wanted and unwanted mail is more complex. That's where a filter program like Mail Rule Manager steps in. You start out by creating rules and then you get to tell your BlackBerry what to do with the message. For example, you could tell the app to create a rule that applies to specific senders, messages with specific words in the subject or in the body of the message, or mail that has an attachment. Then you complete the rule by instructing the manager to delete, forward, send an auto-reply, vibrate, or another rule.

This app is relatively easy to learn, which is good since there are no instructions. The app is also marketed as BlackBerry Filters & Mail Rule Manager on some third-party sites.

How to get it
Available from BlackBerry App World and from third-party sites such as Crackberry. Ajani Infotech. Price: $4.99.

SwooshContacts
$ US

Simple is as simple does. SwooshContacts takes a peek into the standard BlackBerry list of names, phone numbers, e-mail and text addresses, and other forms of communication you use and then reshuffles them.

The original BlackBerry utility acts like a phone book. Your entries are listed in alphabetical order. AAA Aardvark Cleaning service, the company you added to the list just once when you had a veterinary emergency, is going to be at the top. Zebulon Zzfister, your best friend forever and the person you most often call and message, will hold down the bottom of the list. That is, unless you install SwooshContacts. This app adds metadata to your contact book. That means it inserts some invisible but important information without changing its basic structure.

If you use the standard BlackBerry contact list, you will not see any difference. But if you load the SwooshContacts app, your contacts will be sorted: it will automatically move to the top any person or company you have recently communicated with. The more frequent the connection the higher up on the list it will go. Over time, the app will automatically adjust the order based on usage patterns.

And you can manually apply your own ordering system, adding stars or hearts to contacts. The more icons you apply, the higher up on the list a contact will appear.

How to get it

Available from BlackBerry App World and from third-party sites such as Crackberry. Swoosh Software. www.swooshsoftware.com. Price: $4.99.

VR+ Voice Recording
$$$ US

Why not use your BlackBerry as a dictation device to send audio messages or even to record a podcast? VR+ Voice allows me to record a long spoken message and then send it from my phone as an e-mail. Audio files are considerably smaller (and less expensive to send if you're roaming) than are video files you might create using the built-in camera of your phone. A one-minute audio recording using this app was about 120K.

VR+ Voice Recording does a very nice job of recording, storing, or sending spoken messages as e-mails. It's a very nice solution that allows you to quickly send a shout-out to family and business contacts — if they are at a computer.

There is no limitation on the size of the file you record; you're limited only by the amount of memory you have in your BlackBerry. And you don't need to store the file on your phone — it can be deleted as soon as it has been sent.

Now I've written here about using this app as a way to send an audio message by e-mail. You can also create a podcast for upload to Facebook or other social media sites, and you can use the free network maintained by VR+ to send a private message or one you want any member of that service to be able to listen to.

How to get it

Available from BlackBerry App World and from third-party sites such as Crackberry. Shape Services. www.shapeservices.com. Price: $19.99.

3 Travel

WorldMate
Free

On the road again? Got your passport? Put all your essential gels, creams, and liquids in a tiny plastic bag? Checked in with the airline? So far, so good. But there's many a slip between the best-laid plans and a successful long-distance trip.

On one trip that I undertook while preparing this book I faced the following: an on-again off-again strike by flight attendants on the major airline I was booked to fly, a major construction project at the airport where my plane was supposed to depart, a looming general strike at the European airport where I was due to land, and your basic hot summer weather pattern of thunderstorms and high winds. Oh, and a volcano in Iceland.

Was I worried that I would miss my business appointment in Athens? You betcha. Was I better off than most of the other 300 or so travelers headed to the airport that very day? Absolutely. I had WorldMate Gold installed on my BlackBerry and it was delivering me a minute-by-minute update on the status of my flight.

WorldMate is a very professional tool for the road warrior, polished to a boardroom shine. The basic model of the app is free, and it has its appeals: a fancy calendar of your itinerary with a few details like departure and arrival times and gates. But the Gold version, priced at about $100 per year, is — for frequent fliers — the one that will put the wind beneath your wings.

In both versions, you can enter the details of your itinerary in several ways: manually by pecking away at the keyboard on your BlackBerry, manually by typing on the keyboard of your personal computer, or automatically by inputting the airline's reservation code for your flight.

There's even an ultra-automatic version: when you receive a confirmation e-mail from the airline, hotel, car rental agency, or a travel agency you can forward it from your BlackBerry or your computer to an e-mail address at WorldMate and their software will scan the message, pick out the reservation code, and then insert the details into your travel itinerary.

And as this book was being written, WorldMate was testing yet another nifty trick: the program will scan all incoming e-mails by itself and try to spot reservation codes. You'll be asked to confirm, just in case you happen to receive a communication from someone whose name is MXTCPLSX or something similar.

You'll get pretrip notifications of any changes to your travel plans and then reminders and weather forecasts as the day draws near. When you land, you'll receive a welcome message with directions to your hotel or meeting or other scheduled event.

If you are a member of the LinkedIn network (see Chapter 4), you can choose to have WorldMate communicate on your behalf to any of your contacts at your destination. Other features include maps and navigation. You can check several world clocks with one click, and calculate prices with updated currency conversion rates. And if you spring for the golden version, WorldMate will stand by to assist you when things go wrong: alerts with suggested alternative flights when necessary and searchable flight schedules for nearly any route.

JFK - LHR, 8/31/2010
Last Update 07/30/2010

Car.	From	To	Dep	Arr.	Dur.
AA	JFK	LHR	8:30	20:25	6:55
BA	JFK	LHR	8:40	20:35	6:55
AA	JFK	LHR	18:15	6:25	7:10
VS	JFK	LHR	18:15	6:35	7:20
CO	JFK	LHR	18:15	6:35	7:20
BA	JFK	LHR	18:20	6:20	7:00
DL	JFK	LHR	18:35	7:05	7:30
KL	JFK	LHR	18:35	7:05	7:30
BA	JFK	LHR	19:00	7:05	7:05
VS	JFK	LHR	19:30	7:50	7:20
CO	JFK	LHR	19:30	7:50	7:20
SQ	JFK	LHR	19:30	7:50	7:20

There's also a travel directory with contact information for airlines, hotel chains, and car rental services. When you identify a car rental agency or a hotel chain or an airline you can click the name and dial the phone number or go online to their Web site.

You can make hotel bookings with a link to hotels.com built into the program; for airline booking you'll have to find a separate service. Bottom line is that, as polished as this app is, it is still a work in progress. One can hope that the end result will be so good that we'll look forward to getting from Point A to Point B in this complex world of ours.

Best features

An electronic personal travel assistant that doesn't take lunch breaks, personal days, or time off to sleep.

Worst features

With all of the information presented here, it's surprising that you can't make or change airline reservations within the program. You'll have to contact the airline or a travel portal for that.

Some of the automatic updates are not yet perfectly caught by WorldMate. I made a flight reservation to London and it picked up on that. Then I made a car reservation to get me back home at the end of the trip, but the app thought I was still in Merrie Olde England instead of Chilly New England; I had to manually correct the pickup and dropoff locations.

It would be nice if there were a more capable search engine, and nicer if the app was able to make suggestions based on your itinerary or your GPS. Also, the list of airport codes is nice, but once you've found out that LXR is Luxor Airport in Egypt it would be nice to have a database of information about the airport, maps, and a quick link to local weather and conditions.

How to get it

Available from BlackBerry App World and from third-party sites such as Crackberry. WorldMate. www.worldmate.com. Price: Limited free version. $99.95 upgrade.

e-Mobile GPS Companion
$$$ US

Most of us have used a GPS device in a car; they started out as relatively large and relatively expensive standalone devices that came programmed with a set of maps and some information about services along the roads we were driving: gas stations, restaurants, and hospitals. You could update the maps and the information — for an extra charge. Today, though, current-model smartphones include GPS circuitry. To begin with, this allows you to own one fewer device: the phone integrates GPS along with its Web communication and telephone functions.

And the information contained in the smartphone can be easily and automatically updated: if a new pizza parlor opens, it can be added to the database listing. When you find a restaurant you can press a button to call in your order. And if you run into an emergency, you can use your BlackBerry to contact police or a hospital and it can tell you — and the emergency responders — exactly where you are.

In fairness, though, these features are still in the early stages of development. The apps are only as good as the information in the databases they consult, and there are some spots where cell signals do not penetrate. But we're moving forward to solve those problems.

eMobile GPS Companion taps into the built-in GPS chip on advanced models of BlackBerry devices and finds where you are; it can also make a rougher estimate of your location based on the cell towers used by your phone. From there it can tie into Yahoo! to show you a map and its own database of hotels, restaurants, gas stations, and services.

So far, so good. The app found where I was and offered me all sorts of information. Unlike Yelp! and Craigslist, this app uses a database that has been through a light dusting if not a fully professional edit. That's the good news. The bad news is that you still have to pay attention. When I asked for the locations of the nearest banks, I received information about the major commercial institutions. But also on the list was the "land bank," a local organization that buys up unoccupied land to preserve it forever free of development. Well, it's a bank of sorts and it has that word in its title, but it does not belong in the listing of ATMs.

Once you have used the data stream to find yourself and download a map, you can save that map on your phone for offline use. The app can also display a satellite view and report your latitude, longitude, direction, and speed. You can share your location with friends by e-mail or SMS message, and you can dial a listing's phone number with a click.

Best features

It's a relatively inexpensive alternative to a real GPS unit or a full-featured GPS app. And I am hoping that with time the professional editors and fact-checkers will improve the database so that I don't end up lost.

Worst features

It's half a loaf. The database is incomplete.

How to get it

Available from third-party sites such as Crackberry and the developer. e-Mobile Software. www.e-mobilesoft.com. Price: $19.99.

FlightView
$ US

I love flying. It's airports I hate. There was a time, children, when you could show up at the airport 20 minutes before departure and stroll to the gate and on to the plane. (And flying was a semi-formal affair: suits and ties and dresses; no "I'm with Stupid" t-shirts and flip-flops.) Alas, things have devolved. Today you need to devote hours to choosing a flight, studying its on-time performance, understanding its route, and worrying yourself sick about what time it really will get up in the air and then down on the tarmac at its destination.

FlightView is one of a number of apps that bring almost all of the data together in one place: terminals, gates, departure and arrival schedules, and then adds real-time tracking so you know what's really goin' on. The company behind FlightView has been around since 1981, begun as a service agency for airlines and airports. In fact, some of the displays on the monitors in airports and on airline and travel provider Web sites use their technology.

It's simple, and it works: enter the date, airline, and flight number and it will tell you the plans. Click Options and save the information to your BlackBerry calendar, along with any notes you might have about the travel. The BlackBerry app will show if there is a conflict with another appointment on your calendar.

British Airways (BA) 112		
Status: Landed	View:	Details ▼
Departure:		New York, NY (JFK)
Scheduled:		6:20 PM, Jul 13
Takeoff:		7:05 PM, Jul 13
Term-Gate:		7
Arrival:		London, UK (LHR)
Scheduled:		6:20 AM, Jul 14
Landing:		5:53 AM, Jul 14
Term-Gate:		5
*All times are local airport times.		
		Add to My Flights

On the day you fly, check in to the My Flights tab for all the latest news as you prepare to go to the airport. The app can also send you an e-mail or text message with a flight status alert on the day of your flight so that you can know just how enjoyable your day of air travel is going to be.

You can also call up a painfully honestly titled graphic called the Airport Delay Map (not the Airport On-Time Aren't We All Happy Map).

It shows the status of most of the major airports in the United States: normal, minor delays, and major delays. On a stormy day you can watch the little dots change from green to yellow to red. And if you're on the ground and waiting for news about a friend, family member, or business associate in the air, you can view a small map that shows you the plane's location, altitude, heading, and expected arrival time.

The app works well and is reasonably priced — about the same as a bad cup of coffee at the airport. It should be noted, though, that you can also get the same information for free by going to www.flightview.com or www.flightstats.com, or even by just entering the flight airline code and number in a Google browser. It's an extra step, and it is not always easy to read a standard Internet page on a small BlackBerry screen. But like airlines, there is more than one way to fly.

The next step for FlightView will be to add premium features, and that is in the works. I would expect to be able to book or rebook flights, search for alternate flights in the event of cancellations or delays, coordinate with hotel and car reservations, and other road warrior essentials.

This product is not nearly as fulsome as WorldMate, but then again, neither is its price.

Best features

Simple and easy to use, a quick way to keep track of your airline travel plans and hopes.

Worst features

The rest is yet to come. Check with the manufacturer for more updated versions.

How to get it

Available from BlackBerry App World and from third-party sites such as Crackberry. FlightView. www.flightview.com. Price: $4.99.

Google Maps for Mobile
Free

Google is out to rule the world . . . or at least plant a flag in every corner. You know a product has made it when it moves from a proper noun to a verb. The lawyers just hate it: don't Xerox a document or Hoover the carpet. Well, I just Googled the Internet to find and install Google Maps for mobile. And now I know exactly where I am, give or take a few yards.

Big deal, you say: you can already do that with a GPS unit. Well, yes, if you're carrying one with you and it has a clear view of the sky. But the folks at Google have figured out how to pack quite a few really neat tricks into your BlackBerry. First of all, if your BlackBerry phone happens to have a built-in GPS receiver (like many of the latest-generation Bold, Curve, Storm, and Tour models) then Google Maps for mobile can figure out where you are using a satellite signal.

But even if your phone is bereft of GPS, this app can still determine where you (and it) are located: it figures out which cell tower or Wi-Fi router your phone is using to communicate and calculates where you are based on that information. Given a bit of time and a bit of movement, it pinpoints your location more closely. You'll see a map with your approximate location via a big blue dot, and then you can help yourself. You can enlarge the map to see the street grid in your area, or you can enter an address. You can also switch to a satellite view in most parts of the world.

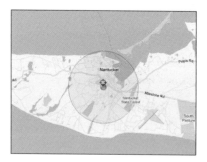

Once you're really pinpointed, in many locations you can ask for Google to give you the street view. I live at the very end of a one-way country lane and yet somehow, someone was there to take a picture of my house. Google's informal internal motto is "Don't be evil." I try to think of it as progress and not something evil.

And you don't even have to type in an address. You've got a phone in your hand, right? Hold down the green "talk" button and speak clearly. I asked for "Hermitage, Saint Petersburg" and in two seconds flat I was back in the USSR, or at least the Russian Republic.

But wait: hankering for a hero sandwich or anxious for an ATM? You can search for a wide range of area businesses as well as museums and cultural sites. Now you know where you are and you have a goal. How do you get from here to there? Why, just ask for directions. You can see them on a map or on a turn-by-turn set of instructions. Are there any traffic jams you should be aware of? Just ask. And in most places you can ask for mass transit help: bus or train details.

Best features

This is one of those wow! apps. Not only is it useful and fun, but you're going to want to invite over the friends and family to show it to them. They might just begin to understand why you carry a BlackBerry. All the time. Everywhere you go.

Worst features

I'll give Google credit for being on the leading edge, but this app could be considered overweight and sluggish. The version I tried demanded about 1.3MB of space on my BlackBerry and is not a speed racer when it comes to performance. But I'll bet Google puts it on a diet and whips it into shape over time.

How to get it

Available from third-party sites like Crackberry.com and from the developer. Download Google Maps on your BlackBerry by browsing to www.google.com/gmm or m.google.com/maps. Or send a text to 33669 with the message BLUEDOT and they'll figure out you want to download the map app. Price: Free.

Kayak

Free

Kayak has an interesting business plan: they *aggregate* information rather than produce their own. On the Web, www.kayak.com looks very much like one of the many other travel Web sites like Travelocity or Expedia. But when you use it to look for an airline flight or a hotel or a rental car, Kayak takes a stroll across the net and brings together in one place the results it finds on travel sites and the directly owned and operated sites of the actual travel service providers. Thus you may find a listing that tells you that a flight from Boston to Reykjavik has several prices: direct from Icelandair, from Orbitz, and from somewhere else. The same would apply if you were looking for a hotel for the night near Keflavik International Airport.

When you make your decision, you'll end up dealing directly with the provider you choose. How does Kayak make money? By advertising and sometimes by collecting a fee from the seller of travel services.

Kayak for the BlackBerry presents a very polished interface, beautifully scaled for use on a handheld device. Any time you start entering characters it assumes you want to fill in a form, which is nice. When you want to enter a date for a reservation, it uses a very simple slot-machine-like rolling selector, which is much easier to use on a mobile device than a tiny image of a calendar month.

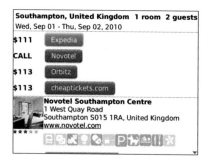

Kayak can determine your position and tell you the nearest airport, hotel, or car rental agency. So hand the phone to someone else in the car, or pull over to the side of the road, and ask Kayak to tell you about hotels in the area or the name of the nearest airport.

Other features include a tab called Airline Fees that presents information — not quite complete, but still helpful — about such things as charges for checked baggage and certain other creative measures taken by carriers in attempts to wheedle a bit more money out of their passengers without being so obvious as to raise their airfares.

The Airlines tab displays the names, phone numbers, and Web sites of the most popular companies. Click the Web address and your BlackBerry will load the browser and head there; click the phone number and you'll be connected. Click Buzz and enter a departure and destination pair and a month. Kayak will display a line chart that shows the anticipated high and low average fares; at a glance you can see the least expensive days to travel. My Flights will store the details of upcoming travel. You can also track a flight that is in the air.

You can find all of these features elsewhere, on individual Web sites. What Kayak has done for the BlackBerry is aggregate them all in one place, in a form that is very nicely adapted for display on a handheld device.

For the record, Expedia, Travelocity, and Orbitz each have what they call mobile sites; you can search for them from Google. But as this book goes to press, Kayak is the only one that has a true app for the BlackBerry making use of many of its special features.

Best features
This travel search engine is optimized for the BlackBerry — easy to use and very helpful.

Worst features
Some of the Web sites that Kayak will send you to make bookings are not optimized for the BlackBerry, and you will have to resort to squinting and zooming.

How to get it
Available from BlackBerry App World and from the developer. Kayak. com. www.kayak.com/mobile. Price: Free.

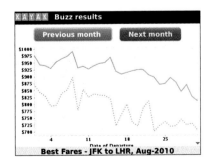

Poynt
Free

You're new in town or just passing through and you need a place to eat. You don't even have to know where you are; Poynt will either use the built-in GPS available on many models of the phone or will take a look at the phone signal and identify the location of the nearest cell tower. That's a whole lot better than pulling off the road and asking some guy at the gas station. If you know where you are or where you expect to be later, you can enter that address as a starting point for searches and for instructions.

But wait, it's much smarter than just a directory. Ask about nearby restaurants and it will display them by name and a short description. Press the Menu key and you can visit the eatery's Web site (if it has one) or place a phone call with a single click. Want to catch a flick? You can ask Poynt to tell you the name and location of nearby theaters and then visit their online listings of films (if they have one) or click to call them. If you have a specific film you want to see, enter its name or choose it from a list and find out just how far you'll have to travel to buy a seat.

You can also search for businesses or people by name or do a reverse lookup of a telephone number. (The phone directory, like all on the Internet, is incomplete — not all cellphones or voice-over-Internet numbers are included, and unlisted numbers are generally, well, unlisted.)

Once you have a destination, you don't even need to bring a map. The listings tie into BlackBerry Maps or third-party maps like Google Maps to show you where you are, where you need to go, and how to get there. Most mapping programs will also make suggestions about the most logical order in which to visit multiple destinations on your list. And if you start to run low on gas while you're out, Poynt can point you to the nearest gas station and even list recent prices per gallon so you can save a bit on a fill-up.

And there are more bells and whistles. Poynt integrates with BlackBerry E-mail, BlackBerry Address Book, and BlackBerry Calendar. So if you make reservations to dine you can enter the information into the calendar, send an invitation and then a follow-up reminder to your significant other and friends, and save contact information for the next big night out.

Poynt is also on the move. It's already available in the United States, and large parts of Canada, France, Germany, Italy, Spain, and the United Kingdom.

Best features

This is an application that one-ups a GPS. It not only has mapping and directions, it ties into a regularly updated directory of businesses. It's like having a personal assistant clipped to your belt at all times. And it's free.

Worst features

Most of the restaurant reviews are written by amateurs. Some seem to know what they're writing about, some don't. Even more importantly, you can't really tell if the chef has enlisted his sisters, cousins, and aunts to post great reviews or if some disgruntled dishwasher is making up stories about mice in the cupboards (or the cupcakes).

And as good as the software and hardware are, they are limited by the quality of the database they check. Not all theaters or gas stations or restaurants are listed, but it's overall a whole lot better than just driving around in your tuxedo hunting for the nearest Chuck E. Cheese.

How to get it

Available from BlackBerry App World and from the developer. Multiplied Media Corporation. http://poynt.com. Price: Free.

RailBandit
$$ US

Despite its name, this is not a stick-em-up: it's an electronic copy of train schedules from many of the major metropolitan areas of the United States. Your subscription allows you to construct as many trips as you want in any of the areas covered by the app; you can see every available train from the current time forward or you can limit the number of trains. And you can ask the system to optimize the selection to show the shortest schedule or the one with the fewest connections.

Although this app does not claim to offer every train system in the country (indeed, when it comes to long-distance routes it only covers Amtrak's major corridors) it is possible to connect between some of the lines; for example, you can construct a trip that goes from Boston to Washington and on to the local Metro subway there to your final destination.

The app does not have much of a search function. The best use of RailBandit is for people who commute daily and want to know the next train for their regular route, or for someone who is traveling to a city and knows their origin and destination stations. You can ask for the day's schedule, or for any date and time in the next two weeks — the app automatically adjusts to take weekends and holidays into account.

On current model BlackBerry devices that include a GPS, you can track your train's progress while you're on board and see if it is on schedule. You can also see your progress on a map. Included in the app are schedules for Amtrak corridors including Boston-NYC-Washington, Empire Service in New York, Downeaster in New England, the Keystoner from New York to Harrisburg, and West Coast lines including the Pacific Surfliner and Cascades.

Big city subway and metro lines are covered in Boston, Chicago, Denver, Philadelphia, and Washington, D.C. In the New York metropolitan area,

RailBandit offers schedules for Metro North, the Long Island Railroad, New Jersey Transit, the PATH line, and the New York Waterway Ferry; not included is the New York subway system, which requires purchase of a separate app. In California, you'll find the BART system in San Francisco, LA Metro, Sacramento Light Rail, and Metrolink.

You can choose which schedules to download to your BlackBerry, and the app does not need to access the Internet every time it is used — only when you ask for a new schedule, an update, or a report on any delays. That makes it gentler on the bottom line for users who do not have an unlimited data plan. And it is also possible to avoid using the data plan on your phone entirely by downloading schedules to your personal computer and transferring them by USB cable to your phone. The schedules themselves are small; according to the company, the largest listing is less than 50Kb, which should allow RailBandit to coexist with your other apps nicely.

Why not just use your Web browser to search one of the train schedules from the train lines themselves? As the maker points out, train schedules don't change all that often; downloading the schedule to your BlackBerry and using a dedicated client like RailBandit is faster.

Best features
Quick and complete: just the facts.

Worst features
The menu and search features are not very user friendly. The maker chose to exclude the New York subway system from RailBandit and sell it separately, which requires use of two separate apps if you commute into or out of the Big Apple.

How to get it
Available from BlackBerry App World and from third-party sites such as Crackberry. Railbandit. www.railbandit.com. Price: $7.50 annual subscription.

𝑅 RailBandit	7:58am
Boston South Station - New York Penn	
Leaves in 17 min	
8:15am-12:16pm	4 hr 1 min
Amt.171	
Leaves in 77 min	
9:15am-12:45pm	3 hr 30 min
Amt.2159	
Leaves in 97 min	
9:35am-1:50pm	4 hr 15 min
Amt.83/93/493	
Leaves in 3 hr 17 min	
11:15am-2:45pm	3 hr 30 min
Amt.2163	

TripCase
Free

There are times in my life when I'm not sure where I'm going and what I'm supposed to do when I get there. I've not yet misplaced my marbles, it's just that I travel a lot. Years ago, I used to carry printouts of my itinerary: flights, car reservations, and hotel reservations among the details. But that was only half the battle: I'd have to call the airline to confirm my flight, call again as I was ready to leave for the airport to make sure my flight was on time, and be prepared to deal with all of the other insults hurled at travelers, including cancellations, gate changes, and unexpected weather delays.

That was before I began packing a TripCase. This nicely polished app for mobile devices comes from Sabre, the holding company that also owns and operates the Sabre travel reservation system used by many airlines and travel providers, the Travelocity online travel booking site, and a number of other related companies. For the moment, TripCase is free to users and sells no products. That will almost certainly change over time; everybody has to find a way to pay the bills.

If it sounds like yet another take on an organizer for busy travelers — like WorldMate or FlightView — well, yes it is. But we all travel differently and have differing needs. TripCase is nicely done, and holds great promise for further expansion. Don't tell Sabre, but I'd even pay a bit for this service. It's a very simple-to-use organizer for the details of your travel that shows the touches of professional programmers.

> **trip⊘case**
>
> **Silversea Silver Whisper Transatlantic**
>
> ✈ BA Flight 112 from JFK
> Departs 6:20 PM on Aug 31, 2010
> view edit delete
>
> 🚗 Hertz Rent-A-Car from London Heathrow
> Pickup at 7:30 AM on Sep 1, 2010
> view edit delete
>
> 🏨 Hilton Southampton
> Check-In at 12:00 AM on Sep 1, 2010
> view edit delete

For example, once you name a trip and enter the first detail — whether it be a rental car to the airport, the flight itself, a hotel at the other end, or a car at your destination — it keeps all of the information in a folder you can easily consult.

If you start with your airline arrangements, it figures out the departure and arrival cities based on the flight number you give it or using confirmation codes from connected partners including Travelocity and other systems. You'll see the expected departure and arrival times and gates, and you'll receive a promise of updates anytime something changes.

Then if you want to add a hotel, TripCase asks if you want it to help by giving you a list of hotels near the current location of your BlackBerry (based on your GPS or cell tower location) or near the departure or arrival airport. The same would happen if you asked to add a car reservation. The folder includes the location of pickup and dropoff sites for car rentals and details about the hotels you have booked including address, phone number, Web site, and maps. The actual tracking of changes to flights begins 48 hours in advance of departure, and you'll learn about cancellations, delays, or gate changes — news in descending order of annoyance level.

One other feature is called TripLog, which allows you to share the details of your trip with family, friends, and business associates. You can also send notes and photos as you travel, tapping into the same list of insiders given access to your TripLog.

Best features

A handsome and mostly intuitive design, head and shoulders over many low-budget apps.

Worst features

Not a worst, just a wish: I'm waiting for the next step and I hope it includes booking and rebooking tools, electronic check-in, and other advanced features for the road warrior.

How to get it

Available from BlackBerry App World and from the developer. TripCase. www.tripcase.com. Price: Free.

Tube Map
Free

The London Underground, almost universally known as The Tube, is one of the more complex urban rail systems in the world. But why am I including this highly specific travel tool in this book? Because this little app is an example of the future of devices like the BlackBerry: help in the palm of your hand. To many graphic artists, the map of the London Underground is an icon, one of the best examples of taking a huge amount of information (270 stations on 11 different lines covering about 250 miles) and making it possible to easily comprehend its structure and trace a route.

Tube Map is a beautifully designed application that manages to shrink down to the small screen of the BlackBerry a window that looks into the huge Underground map, scrolling smoothly from place to place. It's impressive enough to just move your way around the map, but the real utility of this app is to ask it to plan your route: enter your starting station and your destination and tell it whether you want the fastest route or the one that requires the fewest number of transfers.

The result is a text description of the way to go that includes the estimated travel time, number of stations, and transfer stations. It also generates a chart marked on The Tube map, with color dots showing the route and any places you need to change trains. There's also a button to click that tells you the current conditions on all of the lines: congestion, breakdowns, or just the ordinary hustle and bustle.

Tube Map is free, supported by advertising that is unobtrusively placed on some of the screens. The map and programming reside on your BlackBerry and do not require Internet access, which may save some money on roaming charges and also deals with the fact that some places deep down below London may not have full wireless access.

Another feature of the app is Find Nearest Station, which uses the built-in GPS chip in the most current BlackBerry devices. I tried it, fully expecting it would become very confused by my request. Amazingly it came back with the very useful news that the nearest London Underground station to my home and office is at Terminal 5 of Heathrow Airport, a mere 1,981.96 miles. Taxi!

The maker of the app, mxData, already has a New York version available but thus far it only works on the Apple iPhone. In New York, of course, they call their underground a subway; in London, a subway is pedestrian tunnel you can use to go under a busy traffic intersection.

Best features

The setup asks whether you want to be asked before the app goes out onto the Internet to consult the underground traffic report. You can also instruct the app whether you want it to automatically check for updates each time it is started. These are features that would be very nice to see on most apps to help users avoid unexpected data charges.

Worst features

None, really: playing with this app is almost as much fun as winning an all-expenses-paid week in London.

How to get it

Available from BlackBerry App World and from the developer. mxData Ltd. www.mxdata.co.uk. Price: Free.

Yelp!
Free

This is one of those "take it for what it's worth" apps. It's a free listing of reviews and commentary about local services, professionals, and attractions. And the listings are produced by amateurs. There are two ways to look at this. One is to take the view that this eliminates the "bias" of the mainstream media (if such a thing exists). The other is to say that this eliminates the trained eye of a professional writer and a fact-checking editor. You decide.

The good thing about this app and the database behind it is that they include a great deal of data that may help you in the initial stages of a search for something or someone near you. The bad thing is that there seems to be no fact-checking or editing involved and there are both errors and a great potential for mischief if not misdeed. In the class of errors, things like an incorrect Zip code may not make a big difference, nor will spelling "Airport Road" as "Airpot." I found both of these on my first search using Yelp!

More seriously, I asked to find the nearest hospital — something you'd like to be able to find in a real hurry. I started the app, clicked Health and Medical, and the app quickly came up with a few dozen. The problem, though, was that the list did not include the only hospital on the island where I live, the one half a mile from my house. Instead it listed a few 30 miles away on the mainland and then, oddly, went on to include half a dozen guest houses and a veterinary clinic. I ran into the same sort of problem when I asked for a post office near me. It suggested I travel a few hours away to someone's favorite convenience store.

yelp	Hospitals Nearby	
List Results		Map Results

6. Alley's General Store   30.2 miles
State Rd, Vineyard Haven
◻◻◻◻◻ 6 Reviews
Convenience Stores, Flowers & Gifts $$

7. Capeway Veterinary Ho...   47.5 miles
132 Huttleston Ave, Fairhaven
◻◻◻◻◻ 1 Review
Veterinarians, Pet Boarding/Pet Sitting

8. New Bedford Antiques A...   47.4 miles
127 W Rodney French Blvd, New Bedford

I've noted that the reviews are, in general, done by amateurs. Here's an example of a restaurant review: "I really like the ambiance and location of this restaurant . . . However I was disappointed with my meal. I order six Island Creek Oysters on the half shell and found that there was shell in bits in all my oysters. Whoever opened them did a really crappy job. Then the mignonette dipping sauce was incorrectly made and was overly acidic . . . too heavy on the vinagar."

Leaving aside the spelling, I was surprised to see how this reviewer chose to concentrate on two minor details: shells in her oysters and too much vinegar (spell-checking at work) in mignonette sauce. If you use the Web to check the recipe for mignonette you'll find that it is basically vinegar with a bit of shallot or onion and pepper. A few recipes might use white wine . . . with vinegar.

One more review: "The dreaded, moist August heat was seeping into my (irrelevant brand name was listed here) striped top . . . and I was falling down with the hunger coupled with heat exhaustion, wondering if wearing slight concealer had been a bad idea as it was probably creating perspiration droplets on my face." But what about the oysters?

Best features

If you're lucky, you'll find a well-written, well-considered writeup about something you're looking for. Lucky coincidences sometimes make for great meals, great times, and great experiences.

Worst features

You have no idea whether someone else's opinion is appropriate, honest, or correct. And some of the listings are paid ads, not clearly identified as such.

How to get it

Available from BlackBerry App World and from the developer. Yelp! www.yelp.com/yelpmobile. Price: Free.

Cortado Flight Mode
$ US

Stuck in an aluminum can with no access to the world except for the view out the window: that's my life for a good part of each year. Although some airlines are beginning to offer Internet on board, the service is by no means universal or inexpensive and it is designed for a laptop. In other words: not very pleasant to use on a BlackBerry.

But let's get back to the opening scenario. You have a stack of messages that come in as you are driving to the airport and then as you wait in the terminal to board your plane. If you use the Manage Connections utility that is part of the basic controls of your BlackBerry you can click the option to Turn All Connections Off. That disables your phone's Wi-Fi, Bluetooth radios, and cellphone and allows you to use any application on your BlackBerry that does not require communication. You can consult your e-mails, but you're only going to be able to see the first few lines of any you have not yet opened.

Cortado Flight Mode gives you another option. First of all, it will open any new messages and save them to your device memory. Then it will automate the shutdown of your phone's radios to comply with the flight attendants' demands. Once you are in the air, you can turn on your BlackBerry (an indicator on the icon shows that radios are off) and you can read your mail. Note that e-mail attachments are not downloaded. When you land, you turn on your BlackBerry and click Cortado Flight Mode once again; it will re-enable your phone's communication systems and you can resume your normal fully connected life.

How to get it

Available through BlackBerry App World or third-party sources such as Crackberry. Cortado. www.cortado.com. Price: $2.99.

FlightCaster
$ US

The only thing worse than sitting around and waiting for an airline flight is being fed a steady stream of bad impressions from "Hogan's Heroes" by the agent at the gate: "I know nothing!" FlightCaster tries to fill in the huge gaps for airline travelers by assessing the probability of delays for a particular flight; it's at its best about four to six hours before scheduled departure. FlightCaster takes data that includes airline and government data about on-time performance for a particular flight and then adds to it the latest news from the FAA Air Traffic Control System Command Center and the National Weather Service. And then it mixes in any official status reports from the airline itself.

In the version I looked at, FlightCaster was only reporting on flights between points in the United States. According to the company, it hopes to add Canadian and international flights to later versions.

This is a fine piece of work, although you do have to understand how airlines work (or don't work) to use it properly. FlightCaster may report that an incoming flight is going to be six hours late; before you head back to bed, check with the airline to see if they're rolling out a substitute plane or offer a different routing.

The other good use for this app is to find out as much as you can about the history of a particular flight before you make a booking. For example, if Delta's flight from LaGuardia to Tampa at noon is almost always 90 minutes late, you might want to consider a different flight or airline.

How to get it

Available through BlackBerry App World and third-party sources such as Crackberry. FlightCaster. http://flightcaster.com. Price: $2.99.

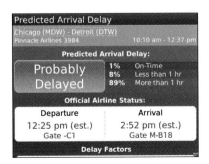

HRS Hotelportal
Free

The HRS Hotelportal includes about 250,000 hostelries around the world. HRS is a German company — one of the larger hotel booking companies in Europe. You can use the built-in GPS facilities of advanced BlackBerry models to find hotels in your vicinity, or you can begin a search by entering a city. Another option: open a search based on an entry in your address book or calendar.

I found their prices and offerings about the same as those offered by the ones most familiar to American consumers, but HRS offers a very quick and straightforward display of information about hotels and their facilities. You can also click a link to make a call to their reservation desk, an option not always easily found at other online services.

Don't expect to get into bidding games like you'll find on Priceline and similar sites. Just the facts and a quick booking engine. Once you have your reservation, the booking confirmation can be sent to you by SMS text or e-mail. If you know what you want and are ready to pick from a list, this portal will serve you well. And you can also use it just for research and try to improve on the price at other sites; just saying, you know what I mean?

How to get it

Available through BlackBerry App World or directly from the developer. HRS Hotel Reservation Service. www.hrs.com. Price: Free.

IamHere
$ US

Well, everybody has to be somewhere, right? But sometimes we don't know where that is. IamHere is a very simple tool that links together the features of Google Maps for mobile (see earlier in this chapter), a screen-capture program, and a connection to your contacts list and BlackBerry calendar.

So with a few clicks, you can

- ✔ Use the internal GPS or other tools in your BlackBerry to find out where you are.
- ✔ View that on a Google map.
- ✔ Send an e-mail that announces "I am here."
- ✔ Record the latitude and longitude on your calendar.

There's nothing here that's not found elsewhere. It's just that IamHere puts it all in one place.

When I head out on my next trip in a few weeks, I fully intend to bother my friends and family with digital photos taken by my BlackBerry and accompanied by e-mails that show exactly where I was standing.

How to get it

Available from BlackBerry App World and from third-party sites such as Crackberry. Toysoft Development, Inc. Price: $1.99–$2.99.

Navita Translator
Free

Parfois, je parle le français comme une vache espagnol. And other times, my French gets better and no Spanish cows are insulted. (The phrase, in French, is an idiom about mangling the language.)

Navita Translator is a nicely polished portal that allows you to enter words or phrases in more than 50 languages and translate between and amongst them. It can also give you an audio readback of the translation in a handful of languages, including at last count English, French, German, Italian, Portuguese, Russian, and Spanish.

What Navita, a Brazilian company, has done here is harness the immense power of two already-developed free computer programs: Google Translate and Bing Translate, from Google and Microsoft respectively. They've designed a nicely polished portal and sized it for the BlackBerry, et voilà: go forth and translate.

You can choose between the Google and Bing versions (in my opinion, Google does a better job) and easily switch languages. And you can cut and paste to and from e-mails and text messages or send your translations to Twitter. The free version comes with an ad banner across the bottom. For a small annual fee you can turn off the ad. Note that the app uses data to obtain translations and pronunciation.

How to get it
Available from BlackBerry App World and from the developer. Navita Software. www.navitasoftware.com. Price: Free.

Does the king have any more unmarried daughters?

Translate with GTranslator

English ⇄ Swedish

Har kungen ha några fler ogifta döttrar?

NAVITA
Portais e BlackBerry

BlackBerry Specialist

NYC Subway Trip Planner
$$ US

Earlier in this chapter I write about the elegantly designed and mapped London Tube app. Here we have a near equivalent for the New York City subway. It's a bit rough around the edges, the map is confusing, and the instructions require some translation. You got a problem with that?

Developed by the same people who deliver the RailBandit app that includes train schedules for many metropolitan areas and rail corridors around the United States — with the exception of New York City — this product handles a very complex system that has an almost impossibly complex set of possible transfer points and alternative routes.

The map itself is downloaded to your BlackBerry and stored there, which means that you don't consume data and you can use the app while you're in a hole in the ground below Gotham and unable to get to the Internet. You can scroll around the complex subway map with 468 stations and click a particular one to make it your origin or destination. Or you can choose one of New York's two dozen lines and routes and explore in that way. And you can save your favorite destinations for quick recall in the future.

Because of the complexity of the system, it can take as much as 20 seconds for the BlackBerry to calculate a route between two points; considering all the calculations going on under the covers, that's not that much. Fuhgetaboutit.

How to get it

Available from BlackBerry App World and from third-party sites such as Crackberry. Railbandit. www.railbandit.com. Price: $7.50 annual subscription.

4 Productivity

Top Apps

- Documents To Go Premium Edition
- Business Card Reader
- Call Time Tracker by Momentem
- Evernote
- ExpenseManager
- LinkedIn
- Nice Office
- SugarSync
- Vlingo
- Xobni Mobile

 Documents To Go Premium Edition
$$$ US

This is a pretty nifty book, full of text, screen captures, and graphics. And to think that the entire project was created on the keyboard of a BlackBerry! Well, that's not exactly true. All of the apps were tested on a BlackBerry and the screen captures were created on that device. But most of the writing was done on a conventional personal computer with a full-size keyboard, widescreen LCD, and the full features of the Microsoft Office suite of software.

But: the very same files that were used to create this book have traveled back and forth from my PC to the BlackBerry for review, editing, and e-mailing. This was all made possible by a suite of apps from DataViz called Documents To Go Premium Edition. (Current versions of the BlackBerry operating system, from OS 4.5 onward, include a basic version of Word To Go, Sheet To Go, and Slideshow To Go that can be used to open, read, and make basic edits to a file. On most BlackBerry devices you'll find those functions in the Applications folder — not the Downloads folder.)

With Documents To Go Premium installed on my BlackBerry, I am able to perform edits on Microsoft Word, Microsoft Excel, and Microsoft PowerPoint files or rename them. I can also create files and save them in the native formats for those programs.

No one is going to say that it is easier to work on the small screen and keyboard of a BlackBerry than it is on a regular computer or laptop, but here's what I was able to accomplish using this app:

- ✔ Jetting along at 30,000 feet (with the cellphone radio turned off to comply with airline regulations) I read and reviewed Word documents for a presentation I was going to make. I also paged through and practiced my spiel for a PowerPoint presentation. And I loaded and updated the Excel spreadsheet I use to keep track of the status of my various projects.

- ✔ A few weeks into my travels in Europe I used my laptop to put together a PDF slideshow of photos. I saved it on the laptop, then connected my BlackBerry to the computer and uploaded it to the media card in the smartphone. Then I edited the slideshow as a PDF before using the BlackBerry to e-mail to friends and family.

- ✔ And as a valuable element of all these tasks, I was able to use Documents To Go Files as a file manager to store and manage fully functional copies of my critical files on the BlackBerry's media card. I live in utter fear of suffering loss or damage to my laptop when I travel; my BlackBerry now relieves me of most of that anxiety.

Key to the value of Documents To Go is the InTact Technology, which promises that any editing done to your files on your BlackBerry will work when the same files are displayed and used on a personal computer. Another feature, added to the most current versions, is support for password-protected files.

DataViz has spread its technology to all of the major smartphone platforms but has done a good job of making the BlackBerry version feel an integral part of the device; it supports the standard menu system and shortcuts.

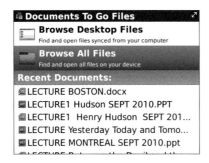

Included with Documents To Go Premium is a desktop application for your computer that helps manage the synchronization of files created on either the computer or your BlackBerry. (You can also manually move files back and forth using the Mass Media Mode that is part of the smartphone itself.)

Also an element of the Premium package is an app called PDF To Go, which allows you to view files saved in that format as well as copy text from documents, perform a Save As, search for bookmarks within the document, and send the file by e-mail. As an example, I opened a PDF of an instruction manual for one of my cameras (a file I carry on my BlackBerry as a backup) and then selected a block of text and copied it to the clipboard. Then I switched applications to the e-mail app and pasted the text into place and sent it as plain text.

In Word To Go, I was able to open, read, and edit files created in the latest version of Microsoft Word. I could adjust the display's zoom size so there was a good balance between the size of the text and the number of lines that could be read at a glance. And when it came to creating a Word file, I could use most of the standard formatting commands (selecting from five common fonts including Arial, Calibri, Cambria, Courier New, and Times New Roman as well as Symbol and Wingdings special characters). The app includes a spell checker and word count, manual and auto creation of bullets and paragraph numbering, and page break insertion.

The Sheet To Go app supports 111 Excel functions. You can sort data and apply cell formatting.

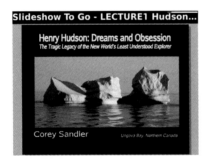

Best features

You can open Word, Excel, or PowerPoint files on your BlackBerry without any desktop or server conversion. Files can be retrieved from the media card or via e-mail, Internet, or wired or wireless transfer from a computer.

Works well as an editing and revision tool for Word and Excel files (and for files created in other programs that save their output in compatible formats).

Worst features

The Slideshows To Go app is the weakest of the group because it does not display most animations, timings, and special effects incorporated into PowerPoint presentations. It works best when there is one image or one page of text per slide.

The biggest downside to this product, though, is the decision by the developer DataViz to offer only the bare minimum of support to registered users. There is no telephone support and less-than-satisfactory online FAQs. Be sure to get a trial version or a money-back guarantee before paying for the premium version of the product.

How to get it

The basic app is included in current versions of the BlackBerry operating system. To upgrade to the premium edition, purchase a download from BlackBerry App World, third-party sites, or the developer. DataViz. www.dataviz.com. Price: $49.95 for premium edition.

Word To Go - LECTURE BOSTON.docx

Unlike the American south or the Midwest or New Jersey, **BAHston** is also a place where the residents do not have any discernible local accent.

Why are you laughing?

There is no accent. It's the other people who *TAWK WICKED AWwD*.

Business Card Reader
$$ US

One of the joys of travel is returning with a stack of business cards; I've come home from conventions with a collection an inch thick. That presents one with several options. You can put a rubber band around them and plan on thumbing through them the next time you want to follow up on a meeting. You can go through them one at a time and enter the details into a contacts program on your personal computer or on your BlackBerry and then synchronize between the devices. Or you can use a program like the cleverly titled Business Card Reader (BCR) to automate the process.

BCR uses the autofocus camera in current advanced models of the BlackBerry to digitize an image of a business card and then applies the proven optical character recognition of Abbyy software to "scan" the image. The result is data that is then fed into the built-in contacts application on your BlackBerry.

It's a fine idea, and the app is well designed. And the underlying Abbyy technology is among the best of its kind, in use around the world. You may sense a "but" coming up, and you're right: but not all business cards are created equal. This app will work quite well on a simple card that uses just text and is logically designed and cleanly printed. The problem comes with artsy cards that use fancy typefaces and unusual designs. The more complex the business card the more likely BCR will misread some characters or erroneously assign a category.

And then there is the proper use of the camera. First of all, this app is only certified to work with the most current of BlackBerry devices — ones that have at least a 3.2 megapixel camera that includes autofocus. As this book goes to press, models that meet these criteria include the Tour 9630, Curve 8900, Storm 9500/9520/9530/9550, and Bold 9700.

You are also advised to turn off the flash, set resolution to high — at least 640×480 — and take photos in bright light (under a lamp or in the sun) but not so bright that there are reflections or distortions. Changing to black-and-white mode may also improve performance. Those are a lot of qualifications, but then again if you are going to scan through a big stack of cards it's not a huge deal to set up the camera properly at the start.

The app will "scan" the image a few times; some complex cards require three or four passes. When the character recognition is complete you hear a tone and see the LED flash.

Even with all the setup, in my experience you need to proofread the scan against the actual card. Watch for number 1s that are read as , for example. Be on the lookout for company names that are d on the card as fancy graphics and ignored or mangled. In ords, use Business Card Reader for the first pass and your own the second. Spend the time to make corrections before you app to store the contents as a new contact or merge it into an contact.

is capable of reading cards in English, French, German, Italian, nish. And Business Card Reader can also take the name and rch the LinkedIn network to see if that person is listed there.

Best features
Not having to type in the information from a stack of business cards.

Worst features
You still need to use the smartest computer in the room — your own brain — to proofread and correct information. The fancier the business card the more likely it will need to be proofed and fixed.

How to get it
Available from BlackBerry App World and from third-party sites such as Crackberry. Shape Services. www.shapeservices.com. Price: $9.99.

Call Time Tracker
Free

Years ago I became involved in the periphery of a legal dispute between two other companies and I had to engage the services of a highly capable, high-priced lawyer to look after my interests. She was also a very nice woman, and she always took a few minutes to ask about me and my family and perhaps about the previous night's Red Sox game. And I tried to be nice, too, except I kept thinking, "She's billing me $150 per hour. That's $2.50 per minute. Family's fine. Weather's lovely. The Sox won. Let's talk business."

One of the reasons lawyers and accountants and consultants charge as much as they do is because of the complexity of managing their billing. They used to keep a log sheet alongside their phone and then their computer and the goal was to assign every possible billable minute to somebody. (The other reason they charge so much: because they can.) Nowadays, much of the work of expense tracking in the office is done by computer software which runs clocks and produces reports all day long.

But what about when a professional is out on the road, away from the desk, equipped only with . . . a BlackBerry? That's where an app like Call Time Tracker comes in.

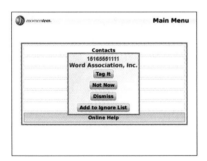

It sits patiently in the background waiting for you to make a call, receive a call, send an e-mail, or receive an e-mail. It turns on a clock that records the event, down to the second, and then as soon as you have completed that task a message pops up on your screen asking if you want to tag that event. If you tag it, the app lets you assign it to a particular contact or a specific ongoing project. You can insert some notes about the purpose of the call or e-mail. And the system can also apply your billing rate to the task. Five minutes and fifteen seconds at

$150 per hour? Why that's $13.13 rounded up by half a penny. You can also add specific expenses and tie them to a client.

And when it comes time for your clients to pay the piper (or the lawyer, accountant, consultant, or anyone else who bills for time) Momentem can produce a report on the screen of your BlackBerry or as an Excel spreadsheet document that you can e-mail to a computer for further processing. A typical report includes a general summary of the total hours in a period, the billable hours, and direct expenses incurred. You'll also see how many incoming and outgoing calls and e-mails were tagged as sources of income. The view for individual clients breaks down time, calls, and any notes you've made. If you've assigned an hourly rate it calculates the bill.

You can also send an instant e-mail to yourself or your contact after each tagged phone call as a reminder of whatever was discussed or to put in writing follow-up actions that need to occur. And the reminder is also on billable time, if you choose.

Best features

Momentem pops up after each time you make a phone call or send an e-mail from your handset, which is a good thing if you are mostly using your BlackBerry for billable activities.

Worst features

There's no way to turn off the app. You can dismiss a call or declare it not to be tagged, but it asks each time a bill might be generated. Help screens are presented in nearly unreadable type. And the product name is spelled awkwardly and there is a different unrelated service online that uses the dictionary spelling.

How to get it

Available from BlackBerry App World and from the developer. Widality. www.momentem.net. Price: Free.

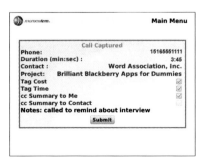

Evernote
Free

Elephants, they say, never forget. And they also seem to be able to communicate what they know to other members of their herd. And thus we have both the concept and the icon for Evernote, a BlackBerry and Web combination that is intended to help you keep track of thoughts, notes, images, and files in a manner that does not rely on a rigid structure. Just make your note — or clip it from a Web page or another app — and save it to your Evernote account. Then later, when you want to retrieve that gem of an idea or that snippet of data or that photo of a business card, just search for it in your freeform file cabinet using tags you applied or words within the note.

You can leave notes in the electronic equivalent of a pile or sorted into folders. But the most impressive part of this app, the function that makes it an exciting productivity tool, is its ability to figure out just what it is you have stored in your account: it can read the contents of a file, even examining an image to pick out words and sentences.

Evernote does all the heavy lifting on its own servers. It can read printed and even handwritten text within images; snap a picture of your notes or a business card or datasheet; and allow the program to read it, categorize it, and make it searchable.

You could forward your airline confirmation (or take a photo of it and send it as an image) to allow Evernote to store the information for retrieval and use. When you're at the meeting at the other end of your business trip you could take a picture of the whiteboard and be able to retrieve either the image or the information written on it.

The freeform uses of Evernote are nearly endless: shop for a car by snapping pictures of window stickers, or do the same with price cards in a shop. And then you come to a wide range of BlackBerry apps that have made themselves specifically compatible with Evernote. You can grab news articles from AP Mobile, for example. (See Chapter 5 for information on that app.) Or integrate the character recognition facilities of Business Card Manager (described in this chapter).

The app and the Web component are offered as a free advertising-supported product although there is a (large) monthly limitation on the amount of data; as this book goes to press you're allowed 40MB per month. A premium service bumps that all the way up to 500MB per month and also adds some additional indexing and searching (including text within PDF files). Think of a blank piece of paper upon which you can write a book, draw a picture, or paste a clipping. Then add a computer-driven scanner that can understand what's there and index it.

Evernote is not alone in this sort of product. On desktops there is Microsoft OneNote and Lognoter PIM; for Mac users there are Yojimbo and Journler. But this particular elephant's memory (also available for iPhone, Android, and other smartphones) is perhaps the most refined. In fact, its performance — and the possibilities it presents — make it nearly unforgettable.

Best features

The best features of this free-form filing and index app are those that make the most sense to you. The app adapts to your data, not the other way around.

Worst features

Not a worst, just two facts: it sends and receives a lot of data, which may or may not present an issue to some users, and some people might have concerns about the security of the information stored at the other end of the pipeline.

How to get it

BlackBerry App World or from the developer. Evernote. www. evernote.com. Price: Free for the basic service; $5 per month; $45 per year.

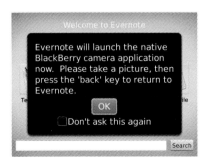

ExpenseManager
$$ US

I travel a lot. Not complaining, mind you. But when I come back from a six-week speaking tour in Europe, or a month-long research trip to Canada I have a headache that is greater than anything generated by jet lag: reconciling my expense report. I carry a travel wallet (discretely hidden within my clothing; any pickpocket is going to have to get very, very personal with me if he or she wants to get at it). That's where my cash and my credit cards and a photocopy of my passport live; most of the time the real passport is back in the safe in the hotel or on the cruise ship.

The other thing I carry around nearly all the time is my BlackBerry, and that is where one of my new best friends lives: Expense Manager. This application is very simple and very useful, two of my favorite attributes in a travel companion. When I spend money — whether it is cash (dollars, pounds, euros, rubles, kroner, whatever) or use a credit card, the next step in my process is to whip out my BlackBerry and open Expense Manager.

There are very few surprises — just a capable specialized database that I can easily keep up to date. The application allows me to create multiple accounts — for example, one for business and one for personal expenses. Or I can create accounts that are tied to a specific project, which is very useful when I am working for more than one client at a time.

Expense Details	
Date	Jul 14, 2010
Description: Yusupov Palace Ballet Recital	
Payment Currency	RUB ▾
Amount Paid: 1800	
Exchange Rate: 0.034019	
Amount: 61.23	
Payment Method	Cash ▾
Category	Entertainment ▾

I can record expenses paid with cash, credit or debit card, or check. In fact, if I want to add a Paid By category that indicates barter by fish I could do that, too. How many fish do I need to give you for a lift to the airport?

At any time I can go to a report screen on the BlackBerry and look at my expenditures, sorting them by date or amount. I can open an entry and read the description I put in for each record. And then at the end of a trip — or any point along the way — I can export the records that are being held in the app. I can save the report to the memory card in the BlackBerry. I can produce a report in HTML format (that's like a Web page) and print it for submission with my expense report or keep a copy in my tax files.

Even better: I can ask Expense Manager to save the information in a particular form called a CSV file (comma-separated values). The data stored like this contains just the facts with few (or no) special codes for presentation. For that reason, the data can be opened and manipulated using many PC or Mac software programs, including Microsoft Excel and many computer-based accounting and banking programs. The advantage here is the ability to import the data into almost any other program on a computer.

Best features

The design is, for the most part, very intuitive. You don't need to adjust your way of thinking to the program. Just enter the date, the amount, the currency, and choose a category. Expense Manager takes care of the rest.

Worst features

I'd like to be able to add some less-common currencies: no respect here for Icelandic kronur, Israeli shekels, Maltese liri, and Polish zlotych, to name a few. And the exchange rates are set at the time of the most recent edition of the application, although you can (and should) manually update the rates at the time of your visit.

How to get it

Available from BlackBerry App World and from third-party sites such as Crackberry. Total Wireless Solutions. Price: $5.99.

Expenses		
Date	**Description**	**Amount**
6/24	Lufthansa 256 JFK..	893.00
6/25	Taxi Athens airpor..	65.74
6/28	Haircut, London	45.53
7/2	Commuter rail pa..	8.74
7/14	Yusupov Palace B..	61.23
Total Expenses :		**1074.24**

LinkedIn
Free

We live in a Facebook, MySpace, and Twitter world, and that's just fine for tens of millions of people who feel the need to chat about the weather, their favorite idol, and the latest star whose face has appeared in a mugshot. Me? I am much more interested in money. By that, I mean running my business and regularly rattling the doorknobs of all of my business acquaintances and partners who might have some work to send me.

That's where LinkedIn plays a part. It's the business equivalent of a social network. It's not a place where you discuss your astrological sign or your favorite hip-hop ringtone; it's a community in cyberspace where you seek to market that most important product: you. LinkedIn has more than 70 million members in more than 200 countries. About half of the members are in the United States, which means half are elsewhere around the world. Either way, that's a lot of possible partners.

The BlackBerry version of the site gives access to a reduced set of features. It works fine to check in on contacts you already have or to respond to an inquiry sent to you by someone with whom you don't already have a relationship. But the more complex work of setting up a profile for yourself is much easier to perform on a personal computer with a full keyboard, a large screen, and a high-speed Internet connection.

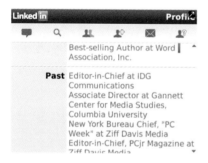

Membership is free (as are the computer and BlackBerry portals to the service). The company makes its money on ads and the sale of optional enhancements. When you join, you create a profile that lists your job titles, skills, and experience. There are sections for a resume of your working career, education, and other background. Once your profile is online, you can invite trusted contacts to join LinkedIn and connect to you; or one of your contacts may invite you to join.

Depending on the settings you choose and how carefully you select the people you invite (and the people you respond to), your listing on LinkedIn can be a safe and secure way to expand your personal brand. Over the years, I have managed to keep track of the comings-and-goings of a number of business associates. More than a few times, the network has allowed me to explore or set up business deals.

The connections grow from your direct connections to contacts to second- and third-degree connections to those who are linked to people you know. In other words, you can find a way to communicate to a friend of a friend, or a friend of a friend's friend. What you have in common are LinkedIn and past relationships. You can also used LinkedIn to research companies. Participating enterprises provide the network with information about their business and sometimes about employees and employment opportunities.

Best features

This site means business.

Worst features

Like much of the Internet, there is no editor involved in this process. Be careful not to rely on information gathered from a LinkedIn profile without verifying it from a primary source. And take care not to list information on your own profile that could embarrass you or cause you problems.

How to get it

Available from BlackBerry App World and from the developer. LinkedIn Corporation. www.linkedin.com/BlackBerry. Price: Free.

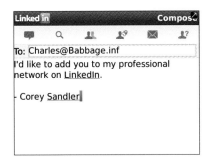

Nice Office
Free

Nice Office is a nice idea — one that bears watching as it matures as a BlackBerry app. Basically, it is meant to serve as an electronic gofer, a service that keeps track of all the activities you perform using your BlackBerry in an effort to help track your billable time and understand better your personal productivity. Every phone call, every message or e-mail, and any other data exchange that goes through your BlackBerry is logged. But that's just the start: you can upload your business's full library of forms and documents and send them from your BlackBerry to your customers. And then there is the two-way synchronization of your calendar and contacts.

Nice Office exists as a three-part solution:

- ✔ First there is the secure Web site that holds a copy of your calendar, contacts, and other files.

- ✔ Then there is the Nice Office app for your BlackBerry that exists mostly as a manager for the synchronization process.

- ✔ In between is a very active service that communicates from your phone to the Internet by e-mail.

A change made to an appointment or an address book listing on your BlackBerry is automatically sent to your Nice Office account on the Web. The same will occur in the other direction. There's no need to plug in a cable or initiate a sync; it's all done automatically.

Another advantage of using a Web site as an intermediary in the system is that all contacts, calendar events, and tasks are automatically stored away from your phone; if the BlackBerry goes missing or breaks, that information can be reinstalled on a new device. (And Nice Office also includes a feature that can remotely wipe clean the memory of a missing phone while keeping the backup files on the Web.)

Now it doesn't take a rocket scientist to understand that for a user who makes heavy use of their BlackBerry this Nice solution is going to use a lot of data. If you are on an unlimited plan or your company picks up the tab, this is not an issue; otherwise — and especially if you roam outside of your home area or internationally — you may need to think twice about the cost of data. (In my case, this is one of the apps where I disable the permission to connect to the Internet when I travel abroad.)

In a larger enterprise, Nice Office can also be set up to perform employee oversight: a manager can check in on the activity journals for multiple staffers from a BlackBerry or on the Web. It can also be used to transfer leads, sales data, and other information amongst a team.

Best features

Putting a regularly updated copy of your contacts, calendar, and essential files on what is promised to be a secure Web-based server is a great protection against loss of data and opportunity.

Worst features

Lots of data is exchanged in both directions, which could generate bills for some users. And some corporate types might be concerned about security, although having that information on a handheld smartphone also represents a risk. I also ran into a problem uploading entries from a Palm Desktop calendar, a situation that is not unique to Nice Office.

How to get it

BlackBerry App World or from the developer. eAgency. www.nice office.com. Price: Free for an individual user. A corporate or enterprise version requires purchase of licenses and subscriptions, priced at $9.95 per month; that version includes a Microsoft Outlook plug-in, no advertising, and an expanded amount of Web-based storage.

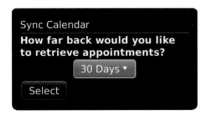

SugarSync
Free

One of the buzzwords of our time is "cloud computing." In some ways it has replaced another invented modern word: "cyberspace." Either way, it means computing or storage or communication taking place somewhere out there . . . and not in the physical realm of your BlackBerry or your desktop computer. SugarSync is a very interesting adaptation of the concept of online storage, extended to the BlackBerry. It is a place on the Internet — doesn't matter where it is located — that is designed to hold backup copies of files for retrieval when needed.

What does this mean to you as a BlackBerry user? Well, it means you have a place in the clouds that can help when you're home or on the road. Let me give two examples of how I might use SugarSync:

- ✔ I'm gallivanting around in Greece or lollygagging in Latvia and suddenly realize that I need a chapter for a book I'm working on. I don't have it on my laptop or on my BlackBerry. And my desktop machine is turned off. No problem: a few weeks ago I had allowed SugarSync to upload that file to its cloud and hold it there behind electronic lock and key. All I need to do now is use the SugarSync app to sign on to my account and download it to my BlackBerry. Then I could either work on it on my smartphone or transfer it to my laptop.

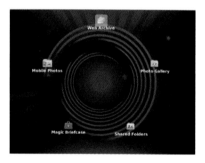

- ✔ I'm traipsing through Tallinn or sashaying through Spain taking tons of pictures with my BlackBerry and with my other two digital cameras. I'm running out of storage space, and even more importantly, I'm getting nervous about the possibility that my irreplaceable photos might somehow become lost, stolen, or scrambled. No problem: I instruct SugarSync to upload the files from my phone (including images I transferred to the SD card from my cameras) and hold them for me up there in the cloud. They will be there waiting for me when I return from my trip.

SugarSync combines secure online backup, file synchronization, remote access, and file sharing all in one. As an individual user, there are two parts: an app for your BlackBerry and a small program that installs on your computer; PCs and Macs are both supported. You can then instruct each half of the equation about what types of files or folders you want uploaded to the cloud, and also set up automatic syncing of some or all files so that a change made at either end is quickly applied to all other connected computers and devices.

The app comes with 2GB of free storage. That's certainly enough to hold many documents, photos, and music files. But the developer is hoping you'll like their product so much you'll want more. One prime candidate: heavy users of digital cameras. The next step up is 30GB of storage, rented for $50 per year or $5 per month; there is a range of other plans that currently maxes out at a whopping 500GB for $400 per year or $40 per month.

Best features

In addition to automatic or manual upload files or folders, you can send data to your account as an e-mail attachment. The system promises to safely deposit the files in your safe storage in the cloud. And they've got a nice icon: a stylized hummingbird.

Worst features

For a product that has a very attractive icon and home screen, the other screens on the BlackBerry are rather dull and a bit hard to read.

How to get it

BlackBerry App World or from the developer. SugarSync. www.sugarsync.com/downloads. Price: Free for 2GB of storage. Larger amounts of space rent by the month or year.

Vlingo
Free

Here's your chance to tell your BlackBerry what to do. The hardest part of using this product is figuring out how to pronounce its name. After then, you leave it up to Vlingo to figure out what it is you're saying. And going the other direction, Vlingo is able to enhance your hands-free use of your phone: it can read aloud incoming e-mail and text messages.

Vlingo uses speech recognition technology; you give your BlackBerry an instruction and the words are sent over the datastream to a computer that attempts to decipher it and execute your command. The technology is pretty advanced, but there are many variables: the quality of the signal, how clearly you speak, background noise, and the complexity of the command. I found that Vlingo was exactly on target about half the time and close enough for me to make a quick adjustment from the keyboard much of the remaining tries: I'd rank it about 80 percent accurate.

And that was just the beginning. As you use Vlingo it trains itself to your voice. When you make a correction from Corney to Corey once or twice it learns from the example. The most direct way to train Vlingo to respond properly is to complete the task you've asked it to do: send the message, dial the phone number of a contact, or open an application.

The standard setup for Vlingo reassigns the left side button on your BlackBerry as the command key. Press and hold it for a second and the app will display a message on screen that it is listening. Say your piece, let go of the button, and wait for a response. Vlingo shows on-screen the words it thinks you said. If the app has heard you correctly you can go ahead and complete the action. If it is not correct, you can fix the command on-screen and then proceed.

It should be obvious by now that this app is still a work in progress. But for most users, including me, there is enough immediate utility in being able to jump directly to a Google search from the home screen by merely constructing a sentence with a verb and a noun: "Google Corey Sandler" for example. (And don't believe everything you see on the Internet, either.) I also found it was effective enough for casual e-mails and text messages, although you will definitely want to go in and edit the words before sending them to a business or professional contact. Again, though, Vlingo promises to improve its recognition as you make more use of its services.

Vlingo can also work with a Bluetooth headset, and in fact this may improve the quality of communication with the voice recognition computer. And in case you were wondering — and I know some of you have to be greatly concerned about this — by default, Vlingo filters words that some people may consider offensive, replacing them with asterisks. Sometimes that's just as effective as the real word, but you can also turn off content filtering and truly speak your mind.

Vlingo for BlackBerry is currently implemented for English only. It is particularly optimized for speaking styles native to the United States and the United Kingdom.

Best features

Your BlackBerry is one giant step closer to Captain Kirk's tricorder. Beam me up, Scotty.

Worst features

Not a worst, but a fact: it takes a few hours of use, spread over however much time you want, before Vlingo begins to recognize your voice with higher accuracy than the moment it was first installed on your phone.

How to get it

Available from BlackBerry App World and from the developer. Vlingo. www.vlingo.com/blackberry. Price: Free.

Title: The memo dictated to Vlingo. |

This is a test of Vlingo.

I dictated all of the words you see you on screen.

It is not perfect, as you can see.

However, the Vlingo promises to get to learn to understand my dictation better as I use it more over time.

Xobni Mobile
Free

The name takes a little getting used to, but the program is a natural. Xobni, in case you haven't figured it out, is Inbox spelled backwards. I prefer to think of this product as my Intern-in-a-BlackBerry-Box. This is a very powerful tool that is a professional snoop: it reads through your existing address book and then sits and waits for every other clue it can decipher about the people you deal with in your business and personal life.

Xobni is like a robot miner, automatically extracting phone numbers from e-mail signatures, anywhere in the body of a message, and from other sources. The information is placed in a contact form: the more data, the more details. For example, if the person sending you an e-mail lists a phone number and a Web site, that is added to the contact. If he also has a Facebook page or LinkedIn profile, the contact will add a photo if one appears on those sites. If she uses Skype, that will show up too. If you communicate using Twitter, the application adds that address and other information it can glean. If a company name is registered with Hoover's or other corporate databases, you can research their financials with a click of the BlackBerry's mouse.

In the first few minutes after I installed Xobni, I received several e-mails and I quickly got to see the faces (and professional backgrounds) of several people who I had previously known only as an e-mail address. When I go to a name, I find not only their contact information but also a list of recent e-mails, calendar entries, and phone calls. One click into the profile of one of my correspondents told me she was a fan of the Boston Red Sox, and now that person has moved way up high in my personal rankings.

And this automated intern can do more: if someone sends you an e-mail without including a phone number, you can use Xobni's Request Phone Number feature. This will generate an automated e-mail requesting their phone number. When they reply, their number is automatically added to their profile. And information can be added to — or taken from — your calendar and to-do lists. You can click a name, navigate to a Schedule Meeting button, send an e-mail inviting someone to a meeting, and insert the name onto the list of attendees.

The standalone version of Xobni for the BlackBerry is powerful enough, catching most every bit of information that arrives on your phone. It works even better if your phone connects to a computer that runs Microsoft Outlook (not Outlook Express). And finally, there is the search function, which brings everything together. Search for "Janice" and not only will Xobni pull up the profile of everyone with that name, but also every e-mail where Janice is mentioned. The features go on and on, but hey: that's what an intern's for, right?

Best features

Never asks for a day off and doesn't whine about having to sort and re-sort the thousands of details in your various e-mails, Tweets, phone calls, and contact lists.

Worst features

By default, it will add to your address book spammers and unwanted communicants. There is no way to tell Xobni not to pick up every possible contact. And there is no way to delete any unwanted addresses either; the closest option is to hide a contact, which leaves them out of sight but not out of mind. I'd like a scrub-and-block feature instead.

How to get it

Available from the developer. Xobni. www.xobni.com. Price: Free version for BlackBerry; subscription for PC.

5 Research and Shopping

Top Apps

- Bolt Browser
- Opera Mini
- Amazon App for BlackBerry
- AP Mobile
- BeReader
- CNNMoney
- English Dictionary and Thesaurus
- The New York Times
- ScanLife Barcode Reader
- Viigo
- WeatherBug

- Concise Medical Dictionary
- Dictionary.com
- Globe and Mail
- Larousse English-French Dictionary
- Navita Sports
- Reuters Galleries for BlackBerry
- Scanner Radio
- SkyMall
- Sports Illustrated
- TIME

Bolt Browser
Free

The Bolt name and icon are meant to make you think of a strike of lightning; it's not quite that fast but it is pretty zippy and it does include a few advanced features, including tabbed browsing (so that more than one Web site can be open at the same time and easily reached).

Bolt (like Opera) speeds things up by routing the Internet through its own servers and compressing pages before they are sent to your BlackBerry. It's a bit like compression that is applied to some digital photos or videos; on the small screen of a mobile phone you're probably quite happy trading off a slight reduction in quality to get a slight increase in the speed at which a page arrives.

Best features

It's faster than the browser used by RIM in operating systems up to OS 5.0, and it offers tabbed browsing.

Worst features

Some pages are optimized for use with the official BlackBerry browser and won't look quite as good in Bolt. But you can keep both apps on your smartphone and switch when needed.

How to get it

Use the BlackBerry's built-in browser to get to Bolt's download page at www.boltbrowser.com and follow the steps. Use the version that's compatible with your model.

To make Bolt the default browser on your BlackBerry so you can open BlackBerry mail, messenger, and SMS links using the tool, you must add another utility.

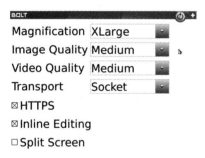

Opera Mini
Free

The Internet browser that comes with the BlackBerry is just another app, and there is no reason you have to use it to get to the Web. Some cellphone companies offer their own browsers and there are others from third parties that you may find faster, easier, or otherwise more pleasing. *Oprah* the magazine has a big O against a reddish background; Opera the browser has a big red O. There are other, more significant differences.

Opera is a full-fledged mini browser, with advanced features including multiple tabs so you can jump from one Web page to another. And your favorite pages are one click of an icon-sized picture away.

This utility — from Norway — is a troll-sized version of a full-featured browser offered for Windows, Mac, and Linux computers and they've done an admirable job of squeezing many functions and settings into a very small package. It's a bit slow to load, but a bit faster than some other browsers once running on your phone.

Opera Mini uses an indirect route to the Web, requesting pages or information through Opera Software's own servers around the world. Those computers find the information or page and then processes and compresses the information before sending it back to your BlackBerry.

In other words, Opera does most of the work of fitting a page to your smartphone at its end. It does not force you and your phone to try to read and scroll through a huge page designed to be displayed on a desktop computer. Pages not specifically designed for mobile phones should look much better, and the overall speed of browsing should be much faster.

The search bar for Opera Mini offers several choices of search engines, although the default is to Google. Therein lies some of the history of the browser, which began as an offering for Telenor cell phone customers in Norway. At first it was sold, then it was free with the display of ads. In its current version, the browser itself is free of charge and free of ads: the company makes its money from ads displayed on Google search pages.

Opera Mini (and Opera for the desktop) introduced or improved on a number of advanced browser features including shortcut keys, skins, and a well-managed set of bookmarks and the user's search history.

As far as I am aware, neither Oprah the magazine nor Oprah the inexplicably successful and wealthy professional celebrity can do any of those things on your BlackBerry.

Best features
It rethinks some of the functions of a browser with its launch icons.

Worst features
Though it may zip along once it's off and running, it loads slowly.

How to get it
Use your phone's default Web browser to visit m.opera.com or www.opera.com/mobile/download. Price code: Free.

Amazon App for BlackBerry
Free

Amazon is amazing. Their empire in cyberspace began as an online store for that most thoughtful and precious of gifts: books. Today you can still buy this and hundreds of thousands of titles from their site, but you can also purchase a lawnmower, sneakers, cameras, and just about anything else, including a BlackBerry device and a cell plan.

The BlackBerry app is an excellent example of distilling a complex Web page down to the essentials. If you're looking to do some intensive research about a class of products or a specific product, you'd still do better by using a personal computer and the full Amazon.com Web site. There are, for example, several hundred thousand items tagged "digital camera" on the site. But if you know a particular model or brand you're looking to buy, or if you can narrow it down to something like "12 megapixel image stabilization" then the mobile site should work well. It displays images of products along with short reviews.

And the purchasing process (including the wish list for items you are considering and the shopping cart for those you have decided to buy) is similar to the full Web site. You'll use the same login and password for each.

I've included Amazon in this listing not necessarily as an endorsement of their business model and customer service, although both are commendable. But I use this app as an example of how a large and complex online service can be reimagined for the BlackBerry.

And then Amazon has gone one step beyond, adding an experimental feature to its mobile apps. It's called Amazon Remembers, and it is a high-tech version of an old parlor trick. Here's how it works: you use the built-in camera of your BlackBerry to take a photo of something you're looking to buy. For example, I had a nearly empty bottle of eyeglass cleaner on my desk; I clicked, sent, and waited about two minutes before an e-mail popped up in my inbox with an Amazon listing for a similar product. Now I'm not going to say that I couldn't have found the product on my own, but Amazon Remembers is a neat marriage of the BlackBerry, high-tech retailing, and a bit of magic.

The system behind Amazon Remembers relies quite heavily on the most complex computer on the planet: the human brain. The photo you take is outsourced to a huge field of humans who look at the picture and make a judgment and a quick search and then use Amazon and BlackBerry to respond back to you.

Although there are other solutions to product search, including apps like ScanLife Barcode Reader (which I also review in this chapter), Amazon Remembers is an interesting nod to the past; Amazon has acknowledged that the system is loosely based on a famous magic trick first performed in Europe about 1770. The Mechanical Turk appeared to be a machine that could play chess, beating many accomplished challengers. It was eventually revealed that a human chess master was hidden within a secret compartment to manipulate the pieces on the board.

Best features

Beautifully adapted to the BlackBerry, a capable and quick reimagining of a huge Web site to allow easy shopping from America's largest online retailer.

Worst features

Where do I put all this stuff I ordered?

How to get it

Available from the developer. Amazon. www.amazon.com/bb. Price: Free.

AP Mobile
Free

My name is Corey and I am a newsaholic. When I am at my desk, I have a Web browser running on a second monitor so I can keep an eye on the front page of *The New York Times* just in case something happens. When I'm on the road I struggle to feed my addiction by suffering through sketchy local television news and reading local publications that are mere shadows of once-great print newspapers.

AP stories form the foundation of much of the news we read in newspapers. (As much as I love the digital world of the BlackBerry and the personal computer, I still have ink in my veins: support your local print newspaper as one way to keep high the standards of journalism.) Consulting the rapidly changing AP "wire" on your BlackBerry is also a way to keep up-to-the-moment on breaking news.

I have to admit a bias: I began my career as a reporter for daily newspapers in Ohio and New York and then moved on to become a newsman for The Associated Press. I used to get paid to write the news and then send it out on the wire to newspapers and radio and television stations. And so I am thrilled to now have AP Mobile on my BlackBerry. I have to admit I miss the clickety-clack of the old teletype machines from the newsroom, but then again . . . they were replaced by computer screens 20 years ago.

The Associated Press is a cooperative, owned by more than 1,500 newspapers and several thousand television and radio stations that use its services and contribute news to the wire. Foreign equivalents include Reuters and Agence France-Presse. AP dates back to 1846; its only American competitor, United Press International, is a mere shadow of its former self, now owned by a branch of the Sun Myung Moon's Unification Church.

When you first run AP Mobile it asks you for your local Zip code and from that it finds the nearest major newspaper with its own Web site; if there is more than one AP member, the assignment will be made by a computer somewhere. The first time I used AP Mobile I was given headlines from *The Boston Globe;* the next time I was given news from the tabloid *Boston Herald.* I entered a Zip right in the heart of Manhattan, hoping to get stories for *The New York Times;* instead, AP Mobile gave me its own NYC local wire.

In any case, changing the Zip code to select a different hometown is useful if you want to follow local news from afar, or if you are traveling and want to know the headlines from the place where you and your app are.

Best features

Quick, automatically updating news stories from one of the last bastions of traditional journalism.

Worst features

News articles are predigested into chunks of about 100 words or less. It's more than a Twitter tweet but less than all the news that's fit to print (or squint). To get more you'll need to read a real newspaper — or at least its full Web site version. Choosing local news feeds is not quite ready for prime time. The process is awkward, and it's a roll of the dice whether you get a major newspaper or a lesser one in the same area.

How to get it

Available from BlackBerry App World and from the developer. Associated Press. www.ap.org/mobile. Price: Free.

BeReader
$$ US

BeReader, also known in some places as BerryReader, is a fully synced Google Reader. Some people will know what that means right away, but others will come to a screeching halt at a wall of technobabble. Allow me to explain: Google Reader is a Web-based aggregator; that means it trolls the Internet looking for keywords or news or entire sites that meet the criteria its users have set. For example, it would keep its electronic ears open for you if you were to say you wanted to know about all things Boston Red Sox.

Now Google's next step was to incorporate feeds from various sites. You can think of a feed as a channel on the Internet. Anyone can set one up, from a lonely blogger pecking away on his keyboard in his basement with endless commentary on the latest trends in eyebrow waxing, to major sources of information like the television networks, national newspapers, and major corporations. There are two commonly used formats for feeds: RSS (Really Simple Syndication) and Atom. You don't need to know any of the technical details of either one of them to use them. BeReader can work with both formats.

The first step in using BeReader is to establish a free account with Google and set up your Google Reader preferences; you can more easily do this on the full screen and keyboard of a personal computer, although it is tediously possible from your smartphone. Google allows you one username and password to access nearly all of its services, which include Gmail, Docs, Picasa, and YouTube.

So with BeReader installed on your BlackBerry you sign in to your Google account and browse through your personalized daily newspaper. The first set of items you receive are just the headlines; click any to read the first paragraph. And then you can ask BeReader to go out on the Internet to retrieve the full story.

Your phone will burn through some data to update its listings. You can adjust it to check regularly for new stories, blogs, and data or wait until each time you open the app, but you can read the material without a connection to the Web after material has been received by your phone. You can add or remove new subscriptions right from the BlackBerry but you have to know the Web address (the URL) of the feed you want; if you sign in to Google Reader on a computer, choose from categories and lists of available feeds. Any changes you make to your account will show up in BeReader on your BlackBerry. BeReader can also be set up to send messages to your BlackBerry to alert you to newly arrived articles.

The app comes with many options for configuration, including choice of color or a traditional black-and-white experience. If you need to conserve data use you can cut back on image download or adjust the time interval between updates. You can choose to see all articles or only those you haven't read, and you can adjust the limit on the number of items stored on your BlackBerry.

Best features

Although this product by its very nature is going to use a fair amount of data and battery power, it has been designed to use compression and power-management schemes to lighten the load.

Worst features

The only good news I see these days appears on the feed from *The Onion.*

How to get it

Available from BlackBerry App World and from the developer. Bellshare. www.bellshare.com/berryreader. Price: $9.99.

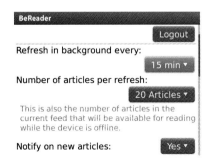

CNNMoney
Free

Unlike AP Mobile, *TIME* Mobile, and even *The New York Times* BlackBerry app, this offering is an invention specifically for the smartphone. And it is a solid, not-yet-famous jewel. CNNMoney brings together some of the features from the CNN newsroom and its corporate magazine cousins *Fortune* and *Money*. (All are part of the Time Warner conglomerate, the world's second largest entertainment company behind only Disney.) Unlike the cable television version of CNN (in my personal opinion), CNNMoney appears to be determined to present facts and stay away from celebrity gossip, talking head bloviators, and other fluff. If you visit CNNMoney from your BlackBerry and you want solid information and numbers, they are off to a good start with this app.

I'll talk about the features that are offered in a moment, but first I want to point out how an app that is designed specifically for display and use on a smartphone is almost always so much easier to use and work with than one that is adapted from a Web page or thrown together from other sources.

CNNMoney is very nicely designed, presenting a great deal of information on a small screen, and its navigation is obvious and easy. The front page is dominated by a display of the major stock market indexes during the trading day. Below that is a scrolling display of the latest business and financial news. Above the indexes is a box where you can enter the name or symbol for a stock or other equity. And then at the very top is a continuously updating display of individual stocks; if you have entered the names of investments, they will be displayed here.

CNNMoney   BMY 26.31   +0.06   +0.23% ☑

| News | My Stocks |

Breaking News
BP agrees to pay $50.6 million fine in partial settlement of Texas City, Texas, refinery explosion case.

Get Quote: Enter stock/company name

Market Index

Last Refreshed: 2:17:48 PM 08/12/2010

S&P	1,082.51	-6.96	-0.64%
NASDAQ	2,187.62	-21.01	-0.95%
DOW	10,315.90	-62.93	-0.61%

Latest News

The second tab of the app takes you to a display of equities and funds. When you install CNNMoney this page comes populated with companies that just so happen to include TWX (Time Warner), RIM

(Research in Motion, the maker of the BlackBerry), and AAPL (that other fruit-based smartphone and computer maker). You can leave those and other stocks in place or you can delete some or all of them and install the companies you want to track.

There's a nice suite of customization options: you can turn on or off the display of market indexes and do the same for sections, including the latest news, company reports, real estate, small business, technology, and personal finance. There are also portals to articles and columns from *Money* and *Fortune* magazines.

The app and the service are provided at that most pleasant of financial levels: free. When I used the product there was no advertising or subscription plans; as with many other products in this brave new world of smartphones, at some point they're going to have to bring in some money to CNNMoney.

Best features

This very good service pushes the latest financial information right to your BlackBerry. The developer does a very good job of warning users about the possibility of incurring unexpected bills if you do not have an unlimited data plan or if you roam outside of your home area.

Worst features

Not a worst, just a suggestion: it would be nice to be able to add the number of shares and purchase price for equities you own so that the My Stocks page allowed you to track your portfolio.

How to get it

Available from BlackBerry App World. Cable News Network LP, a Time Warner Company. www.money.cnn.com. Price: Free.

CNNMoney	ED 47.99	+0.35	+0.73%
News	My Stocks		
Add Stock: ed			
Last Refreshed: 1:34:19 PM 08/12/2010			
T	26.71	+0.15	+0.58%
ADP	39.89	-0.51	-1.26%
BPRCX	11.16	+0.03	+0.27%
BMY	26.35	+0.10	+0.38%
CVTCX	27.99	-0.47	-1.65%
CLX	64.44	-0.19	-0.29%
ED	47.99	+0.35	+0.73%

English Dictionary and Thesaurus
$$ US

English Dictionary and Thesaurus: an electronic version of a dictionary, presented in a Web-like format with links to other definitions, based on a rethinking of the way our language works. This product is built upon WordNet, a lexical database of the English language that was begun in 1985 at Princeton University and is still being enhanced. The research project looked into the way words are related to each other, which is a bit different from the way old-school dictionaries focus on word origins. The idea was to help enhance things like artificial intelligence and natural language processing. "Can you hear me now, Hal?"

Under the covers: nouns, verbs, adjectives, and adverbs are grouped into sets of cognitive synonyms (synsets), each expressing a distinct concept. By definition, then, it includes a thesaurus: synonyms (words with similar meaning) and antonyms (words that mean the opposite). It contains more than 1.6 million American and British English words and 300,000 links amongst them.

If you look up "office" you will get a basic but usable meaning: a place of business where professional or clerical duties are performed. But then you proceed to More General meanings, and here you will find clickable links to Place of Business and Business Establishment. And from there, More Specific meanings: box office, main office, home office, shipping office.

sesq

sesquipedalia
noun   1 entry

sesquipedalian
adjective 2 entries

sesquipedalian
noun   1 entry

sesquipedality
noun   1 entry

sess
noun   1 entry

sessile
adjective 2 entries

sessile polyp
noun   1 entry

sessile trillium

Further down the screen you find more words and phrases, some of which are synonyms and some of which are less directly related: agency, bureau, and authority, for example. Keep going to specific examples like the National Weather Service, the Comptroller of the Currency, and the U.S. Government Printing Office.

Let's take the very basic word "dog" (a domesticated animal of the genus Canis). The researchers, in their rethinking, give us things like hypernyms (superordinate or more generic version of the word, like canine) and hyponyms (subordinate words that are more specific, like Wirehaired Fox Terrier), and coordinate terms that include the word in question, like Shetland Sheepdog. You also have holonyms (something that is related by being a part of the whole word). For example, a hat is a holonym for various parts like its brim and crown. And meronyms (parts of a larger whole). Brim and crown are meronyms of hat.

I'm going to stop here before I digress too far; digressions are the very nature of the Web and at the heart of WordNet. But I will warn you that you will also find troponyms and entailments for verbs and root adjectives for adverbs. In other words, when you look something up within the English Dictionary and Thesaurus on your BlackBerry (or if you go to the source at www.wordnet-online.com) it's a bit like following Alice down the rabbit hole.

Best features

When you install the app, you are given the option to store 26MB of dictionary files on your BlackBerry's internal SD storage card rather than on the device itself, which keeps more space available for apps. Once application data is downloaded the dictionary data is all stored on the device and it does not go out to the Web on its own.

Worst features

The user interface, although very attractive, could use a bit of polish. You should be able to jump right to another definition without having to back up and erase the previous entry.

How to get it

Available from BlackBerry App World and from third-party sites such as Crackberry. Chocolate Chunks Apps. www.chocolatechunkapps. com. Price: $5.99.

adjective:

everyday mundane quotidian
   routine unremarkable
      workaday :

found in the ordinary course of events; "a placid everyday scene"; "it was a routine day"; "there's nothing quite like a real...train conductor to add color to a quotidian commute"- Anita Diamant

The New York Times
Free

They used to call the venerable *New York Times* "the old gray lady." The newspaper is still old, but nowadays she's a pretty hip and colorful gal. First came color photos in the print version of the paper, read by about one million people during the week and more on Sunday. And then came full color and video and special features in the online version of the newspaper, at www.nytimes.com. *The Times* is the home page on the computer in my office. *The New York Times* Mobile is now the news delivery app of choice on my BlackBerry.

The New York Times Mobile, in its BlackBerry version, takes the online newspaper one step further: it recasts the front page into a clickable list of headlines and reformats the stories themselves into easily read snippets.

The equivalent of the front page in the mobile edition is Latest News. Here you see a list of stories, accompanied in most cases by a color photo. Click any of them and you are taken to a nicely formatted article. To go deeper into the paper, click the BlackBerry menu button. There the choices include Business, Technology, Most E-mailed, and More Sections. That last choice opens up to all the news that's fit to read on a mobile device, including World, Politics, Opinion, Sports, Arts, Books, Movies, Fashion & Style, and Dining & Wine.

The New York Times

- Latest News
- World
- U.S.
- Politics
- N.Y. / Region
- Business
- Technology
- Science

As this book goes to press, both the Web and mobile versions are free. The Web version includes advertisements of all sorts — banners, animated thingies, and just about every other sort of eye grabber thus far invented for the Internet. The mobile version has not yet been colonized by ads, although there are Click Here links to subscribe to the print version, which seems a bit counterintuitive.

But the bean counters at *The Times* have announced plans to institute some sort of a subscription fee for the newspaper in 2011. There may be a free version for subscribers to the print edition, or there may be a limited free version for casual readers and fee-based access for those who visit frequently. The mobile version includes the full text of most stories. Special features include blogs that are exclusive to the electronic versions.

You can search *The New York Times* movie reviews, get stock quotes and market information, and view the five-day weather forecast for your Zip code. Advanced feature include customizable news tracker alerts that allow you to follow particular keywords or names.

Don't forget that using the electronic newspaper will require downloading a lot of data; make sure you have an unlimited data plan or are willing to pay for bits that flow your way.

Best features

It's *The New York Times,* not some unedited newsblog or computer-guided aggregation of random stories. There are editors involved.

Worst features

There are still some bugs in the programming, including flaky behavior when you try to go back a page. The old gray lady will call the techies and all will be well eventually.

How to get it

Available from BlackBerry App World and from the developer. The New York Times. From your browser (http://m.nytimes.com) or send a text message from your BlackBerry to 698698 with the following message: **bb install**. Price: Free.

The New York Times

Latest News	Last Update: Moments ago
President Obama on Thursday spoke with	

Contador Retains Tour Lead
Alberto Contador retained the yellow jersey despite a challenge by Andy Schleck on

Spies, Spider Venom and Sex Appeal
In "Salt," Angelina Jolie is the prime special

Failure to Communicate
A masking tape line down the middle of the dorm room? Texting beats talking.

ScanLife Barcode Reader
Free

I love getting new toys: the latest BlackBerry, the snazziest laptop computer, the tiniest high-resolution digital camera, and other essentials of life. It's shopping I hate. I'm always worrying that somewhere else I can get a better price or a better product. Some of that anxiety has been relieved by the Internet, where it is easy to compare prices amongst online sellers. But what should I do when I'm out in the real world, strolling the aisles of a store? So many choices, so little information. You could try flagging down a clerk; unless you're very lucky he or she will know no more than you could read for yourself on the package in your hand.

One answer, and it's a beauty, is to whip out my BlackBerry and load the ScanLife app. With one click, you use your phone's built-in camera to take a snapshot of the barcode on the product; a few seconds later, ScanLife sends back a report. Depending on the product, you'll see prices at major online retailers, reviews, and product details. Click one of the links and you'll be able to read the more fulsome information available at places like Amazon.com or Buy.com, and you may also find less expensive or better alternatives.

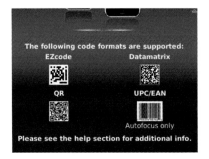

But wait, there's more. Have you noticed barcodes appearing in advertisements in magazines and newspapers? ScanLife (and a few other, similar, but not quite as polished products) makes use of your BlackBerry's camera to send an image of one of the ubiquitous barcodes all around us. These include EZcode, Datamatrix, and QR symbols, which are postage stamp–sized paint splatters. And if you have a BlackBerry with an autofocus lens (this includes many of the most current models) you can also scan the larger UPC code, made up of thick and thin bars and a set of numbers.

The image is received and decoded by ScanLife, and a message is sent back to your phone. Depending on decisions made by the owner of the barcode, you may be able to do even more than just research the price. The code may lead you to a Web page with more information including videos, allow you to send a text message or make a phone call to the company's sales or customer service department, or enroll you in a contest or a mailing list. And ScanLife will maintain on your phone a history of the bar codes you have checked out. This allows you to peruse the offerings in a store and then return to your home or office to do more research before making a buying decision.

ScanLife is free to BlackBerry users; they make their money charging manufacturers fees to produce and register bar codes. But you need to be aware that you will be using your phone's data plan to send each scan and receive each response; be careful if you do not have an unlimited data plan or if you are roaming internationally. And then go forth and shop.

Best features

It's free and it's almost impossible not to save money or shop more intelligently by scanning product codes before you get to the cashier.

Worst features

I may have to actually buy something now.

How to get it

Available from BlackBerry App World and from the developer. ScanLife. www.scanlife.com. Price: Free.

Viigo
Free

Off Viigo and into the amazing universe of newsfeeds, blogs, sports and stock updates, flight schedules, audio podcasts, and nearly all of the little bits of information that define the modern life. It's kind of like programming your own cable television network, only without the cable.

Viigo is a very smooth, nicely designed aggregator of data. It comes stocked with many of the more popular RSS (Real Simple Syndication) and other information feeds. Even more importantly, it allows you to customize the list by deleting or adding more sources from the built-in listing. And you can also insert your own streams of information by entering the address for RSS feeds.

This is all stuff that is out there on the Internet. You could get the information by loading the BlackBerry browser and going to a Web site. You can load an RSS reader. And you can go to a blog directly. What Viigo does is aggregate all of the information you choose to keep track of. It gives you the headlines and a snippet of its content, and then you can choose to read the full article. You can also send what's on your screen by e-mail to a friend or colleague; they'll receive a message with a clickable link that takes them onto the Internet and to the page with the article.

When you load Viigo, you'll see a listing of all the feeds you have asked it to follow. To the right of each source's name you'll see a number telling you how many current articles are waiting for you to read for the first time; when you open some channels, individual entries will also have red stars to let you know what's new in your personal universe.

$50. Free. Click. Any Questions?	*viigo*
Home ⟩ Channels	
▸ :: What's New in Viigo	20
▸ BBC News	World	Full Feed	25
▸ BlackBerry Cool	19
▸ CrackBerry.com blogs	23
▸ Engadget	21
▸ Financial Post - FP Trading Desk	15
▸ Montreal Events Concerts	Upco...	0
▸ Popular Science - Read PopSci	10
▸ Reuters: Business	21
Montreal Events Concerts	Upcoming Events in Montreal, QC - Eventful	

As befits a well-designed app, Viigo allows you to use it in the way that is most comfortable for you. You can go back to the main screen and choose channels one at a time, or you can open any individual channel and then use N (for next) or B (for back) to move through your available choices. T is for top of the list.

As first installed on most current phones, Viigo limits each channel to 25 articles and the total number of stored articles to 500. But you can increase either number if you want; the practical limit is about 1,000 articles, and then Viigo will clean house by throwing away the oldest snippets.

Viigo updates itself each time it is loaded, and you can also make settings to turn on auto-update or set a specific schedule for refreshing the list. You can choose to have Viigo run in the background (which can devour data even when you're not using the app) or only when you load the app. Of course, the obligatory warning: if you don't have an unlimited data plan or if you are roaming outside your home area, be aware that use of Viigo could generate large and painful bills from your cellphone provider.

If there were any doubt about how valuable it was to users, that ended in 2010 when the company was purchased by Research in Motion, the maker of the BlackBerry. RIM has not announced its specific future plans for the app, but we can assume it will become part of the standard package for the device.

Best features

It feels like a product that was designed specifically for the BlackBerry, rather than one that was reengineered and squeezed down to fit.

Worst features

Finding a way to force myself to step away from the phone and get back to work.

How to get it

Available from BlackBerry App World and from the developer. Viigo. www.viigo.com. Price: Free.

To be honest, when Toshiba's 10.1-inch AC100 smartbook was revealed last month it looked like one nice clamshell, but we're

WeatherBug
Free

Everyone complains about the weather . . . and this app will not make the rainy days and the storms go away. But it is one of the more detailed weather reporting and forecasting tools available for those of us without an advanced degree in meteorology (and that includes most of the "weather forecasters" on your local TV).

WeatherBug is a company that provides live weather data to about 85 television stations in the United States as well as schools, museums, and other entities that have a need to know what's coming over the horizon. It has its own network of more than 8,000 weather stations in the U.S. and also ties into networks of reports from around the world, including airport and government agencies.

The app is available in a free version that includes some advertising and a less-than-full but still quite expansive set of features. It all begins with your current location, which can be determined by your BlackBerry using the built-in GPS of most current models (or you can enter the name of your location or its Zip code).

You can drill down a bit for hour-by-hour and seven-day forecasts. There's a link to a current radar for your immediate area and to a regional display. You can get a report from nearly anywhere in the world large enough to have a weather station by entering its name in a screen of the app. Or you can display a map of the world and move around on it using your BlackBerry's trackball or trackpad.

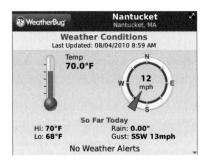

And then your BlackBerry is linked to the WeatherBug server so that any time the National Weather Service issues an alert for your current GPS location it will come through to your phone, even if the WeatherBug app is turned off.

The service even has its own team of meteorologists who can be summoned to appear on your BlackBerry screen to deliver a video report on national and regional conditions. You can also view snapshots and time-lapse animation of weather conditions from more than 2,000 weather cameras in the U.S.

And then there is the Elite version, which drops the ads and includes some more features for less than the cost of a very cheap umbrella. This version adds real-time weather alerts using BlackBerry push services, sending information to your e-mail inbox or home screen. It adds the current temperature next to the time that is displayed on the home screen of your BlackBerry. Also included are enhanced contour weather maps with ten overlays: temperature, radar, humidity, pressure, wind speed, forecast high and low, satellite, National Weather Service alerts, and regional lightning strikes.

Best features

The best feature about this app could also be its most threatening one if the app's maker hadn't done a good job of warning users. In the standard setup, WeatherBug will push weather alerts and updates to your phone as they occur; the average size of a weather update is 20K, an alert just 1K. If you're on an unlimited data plan, that's no problem. If you're not, or if you roam out of your home area or internationally, you're going to want to turn off the pushed alerts. WeatherBug allows you to do this from the Options menu.

Worst features

The Escape key on the BlackBerry does not bring you backwards one screen, but instead to an exit screen for the app.

How to get it

Available from BlackBerry App World and from the developer. AWS Convergence Technologies, Inc. www.weatherbug.com. Price: Free for basic version; $4.99 for Elite.

Concise Medical Dictionary
$$ US

"Doctor, I'm pretty sure I've got an acute flare-up of Ekbom's syndrome. Or perhaps the onset of peripheral neuropathy. I think it may be related to a deficiency in pteroylglutamic acid. Yes, my legs are twitching. That's what I just told you. Why am I calling you? Well, you're the doctor, not me." You've got to feel just a bit sorry for modern physicians these days. Patients have the Internet at their fingertips where they enter a symptom and shop for a diagnosis. There are also uncounted numbers of blogs, talk shows, and medical dramas on their computer and television screens.

And now this: the Oxford Concise Medical Dictionary loaded on the BlackBerry and ready to provide a short plain-language definition of more than 10,000 terms, symptoms, and conditions. This is a dictionary, not an automated diagnosis system: you enter a word (just the first few letters will advance you to the section) or scroll through the listings.

The app can install all of its definitions on your BlackBerry or just its list of terms and then allow the phone to reach out wirelessly to retrieve the data. Users who do not have an unlimited data plan or who are roaming away from their home area need to be aware of how the app works.

"Yes, doctor? Münchausen's syndrome? Please. You can't make this sort of thing up."

How to get it

Available from BlackBerry App World and from third-party sites such as Crackberry. Developer: Mobile Systems. www.mobisystems.com. Price: $9.99.

Concise Medical

foramen
n.
(pl. **foramina**)
an opening or hole, particularly in a bone. The **apical foramen** is the small opening at the apex of a tooth. The **foramen magnum** is a large hole in the occipital bone through which the spinal cord passes. The **foramen ovale** is the opening between the two atria of the fetal heart, which allows blood to

Dictionary.com
Free

What would Samuel Johnson have done in 1755 if someone had asked for the definition of the Internet? It certainly was not in his book of English language words, the model for what we now know as the dictionary.

The Dictionary.com application is a simple, specialized piece of software that allows you to look up the meaning of a word, hear it pronounced in standard English, and switch over to a thesaurus for synonyms and antonyms. Quite a preternatural piece of prestidigitation when you think about it. You should know that Dictionary.com delivers exactly what you would expect from a product of its name: an electronic version of a standard dictionary. It is not a reengineered compendium of bons mots and ordinary speech; earlier in this chapter I discuss the English Dictionary and Thesaurus that is based on the WordNet project from Princeton University. That's not what you'll find with Dictionary.com: this is an app that Samuel Johnson and Merriam and Webster would immediately apprehend.

You can get the same information by using your BlackBerry browser and going directly on the Internet to www.dictionary.com but this neat little app is, as the British would say, purpose-built. And quite nifty, I might add. In fact, I'm gobsmacked. Stop me before I synonymize any further.

How to get it

Available from BlackBerry App World and from the developer. Dictionary.com LLC. http://dictionary.reference.com/apps/blackberry.

Globe and Mail
Free

The whole world does not revolve around the United States of America. But you knew that already, right? You are using a smartphone designed and marketed and considered the pride of . . . . Canada! Up in Canada they have radio and television and newspapers, too. And its largest circulation national paper is the *Globe and Mail,* which is a generally serious and professional piece of journalism. The morning paper is published in separate editions in six cities: its base in Toronto as well as Halifax, Montreal, Winnipeg, Calgary, and Vancouver.

It was the development of electronic distribution that allowed the production and distribution across the world's second largest country. Canada is larger in square miles (or square kilometers) than China and the United States, with only Russia spreading over more land.

With the arrival of the Internet and after that the spread of smartphones, it was only natural that the *Globe and Mail* would arrive on the Web and then on the BlackBerry. What you get is very Canadian: solid and unpretentious with a nice sense of humor. There is a great deal of news about politics and events in Canada, but the international coverage is also first-rate. If you live in Canada, travel to Canada, or are just interested to see how the world looks from up north, this is a good service.

The app is a wee bit slow on the download, but when you get what you ask for, it's as solid as a Canadian maple.

How to get it
Available from BlackBerry App World. Globe and Mail. www.theglobeandmail.com. Price: Free.

Larousse English-French Dictionary
$$$ US

La langue française est très belle et facile à apprendre, oui?

That's what my teachers in high school and college told me, and I've repeated it often as I travel the world: the French language is very beautiful and easy to learn. Oui?

Give the Larousse English-French Dictionary a word in English and it will come up with the French equivalent. Simple words are given just a definition; more complex words come with examples of usage. It is truly amazing to have so much packed into such a small package. But they could have gone further: there is a pronunciation key, but no audio to help untangle your tongue. For that you need a talking translator, available for purchase from HNHSoft and from a number of other providers for the BlackBerry.

It also is nowhere near as savvy as some other electronic utilities. If you type in a word and spell it incorrectly, it won't suggest the correct spelling; it will merely deliver a computer version of a Gallic shrug.

And Larousse, though it is the gold standard for French, is not as hip as it could be. It lacks many modern terms (for example, French Web sites for the BlackBerry offer service de déblocage). Larousse hasn't a clue and neither did I until I thought about it for a while. Déblocage comes from débloquer, which means "to get going again" or in another sense, to "unfreeze." Et voilà: I realized it meant to "unlock" a phone.

How to get it

Available from BlackBerry App World and from third-party sites such as Crackberry. HNHSoft. www.hnhsoft.com. Price: $19.99–$24.99.

Translation

obtenir

obtenir [40] [ᵒᵖᵗᵉⁿⁱʳ]
vt.
1. to get , to obtain ; **obtenir qqch de qqn** to get sthg from sb ; **obtenir de faire qqch** to get permission to do sthg ; **obtenir qqch à ou pour qqn** to obtain sthg for sb ;

Navita Sports
Free

A good athlete is someone who has mastered a particular skill and is able to repeat it and adapt it on demand. Navita Sports is a work in progress, but it deserves noting here because it does one thing particularly well: delivering easy-to-read, well-organized information about sports. To be precise, this Brazilian company has launched its product with sports that are of particular interest in its part of the world: Formula 1 car racing, professional football (what Americans call "soccer"), and professional tennis. During the 2010 World Cup it added coverage of that event with full details of bracket-by-bracket competition.

Game times are based on your local time zone, and interfaces are available in English, Portuguese, and Spanish in the first release. It is reasonable to hope that Navita (or someone else) will build on this platform to add major pro baseball, football (American style), basketball, hockey, and perhaps competitive text-messaging. In the meantime this is a model for clear and concise presentation of data on the small BlackBerry screen.

The free version comes with an ad banner across the bottom. For a small annual fee you can turn off the ad.

How to get it

Available from BlackBerry App World and from the developer. Navita Software. www.navitasoftware.com. Price: Free.

Reuters Galleries for BlackBerry
Free

A picture is worth, they say, a thousand words. And this app, from the Thomson Reuters wire service, delivers hundreds of eye-popping and mind-engaging pictures to your BlackBerry each day.

The Reuters news service dates back to London in 1851 where it was one of the first electronic information providers; it delivered stock market quotations and snippets of news to subscribers. In 1865, Reuters was the first organization to report the assassination of Abraham Lincoln in London. The modern incarnation, Thomson Reuters, is now an American company specializing in business information. But it also distributes general news and photography.

This very simple app gives you galleries of each day or week's most compelling photography. Captions provide a bit of detail, but it is the pictures that move us. There is nothing to configure. All you do is load the app and choose any of the current galleries of photos and then move through them.

After I've read *The New York Times,* consulted AP Mobile for breaking news, and read a bit of *TIME* magazine for context, I turn to Reuters Galleries to satisfy my mind's eye with pictures. You can proceed through the photo galleries at your own pace, stopping to study an image for details or to marvel at the photographer's skill. If a picture is worth a thousand words, then the images sent to your BlackBerry by Reuters are worth millions: they are gems of photojournalism and they help us better understand our world.

How to get it
Available from BlackBerry App World. Thomson Reuters. Price: Free.

Scanner Radio
$US

Before cellphones, before Internet, before almost everything we hold dear and near there was a nearly secret fraternity of geeks who managed to obtain access to police, fire, and emergency radio broadcasts. It was sometimes thrilling — a fire, an ambulance dispatch, a major crime — and it was sometimes mind-numbingly boring. And it was never easy: it required an expensive radio receiver and an antenna and at first you had to know the frequency to tune to. Later models were called "scanners" because they could troll across the radio frequency and latch on to whatever they could hear.

But today, your BlackBerry can use a cellphone datastream to access the Internet to browse the radio waves. The recent progress of technology is summed up in that sentence.

Scanner Radio (also known as BB Scanner) accesses a Web site called www.RadioReference.com and uses your phone's GPS or cell tower locator to find nearby signals. Or you can choose a specific signal: I can sit in Massachusetts and listen to emergency radio in Chicago or Reno or Australia.

I am much too busy to keep the scanner running all the time in the background. But if I hear the scream of sirens in my neighborhood, or if I learn about major news in a distant city, I turn on my Blackberry-to-Web-to-emergency services scanner and listen in on events as they happen. It's still sometimes thrilling and sometimes boring. But it is always neat.

How to get it
Available from BlackBerry App World and from the developer. BB Scanner. www.bbscanner.com. Price: $4.99.

SkyMall
Free

Where do they find this stuff? For all of us who have been trapped on an airliner with nothing to read and no way to go online, the SkyMall catalog has always been worth consulting. I mean, where else are you going to find essential products like a pump-action mini-marshmallow shooter with an LED sight? Or a desktop fan in the shape of an alligator and a set of ear muffs with ultra-sensitive microphones and an amplifier that allow me to listen in on conversations behind my back and across an open field? And I had no idea I needed a King Richard Throne Seat for my office bathroom! Yes, the timeless symbol of Richard the Lionhearted is inlaid inside an incredibly detailed heraldic toilet seat crafted from clear, easy-to-clean resin. Only $69.95 if I act today!

I'm not endorsing this store or these particular products. But this is an example of an app that bridges the gap between a physical store (in this case, a printed catalog that sits in the seatback compartment on an airliner) and the BlackBerry in your hand.

If SkyMall has something you need, or at least want (a baseball signed by Hank Aaron, complete with a certificate of authenticity that tells the world that you bought this from a legitimate dealer without ever having met Hammerin' Hank), then this is the place to go. Now if you'll excuse me, I've got to go measure my neighbor's dog for an embroidered Boston Red Sox jersey.

How to get it
Available from BlackBerry App World and from the developer. SkyMall. www.skymall.com. Price: Free.

Description
King Richard Throne SeatThe timeless symbol of brave Richard the Lionhearted is inlaid inside this incredibly detailed heraldic toilet seat crafted from clear, easy-to-clean resin. Gold-tone fleur-de-lis

Sports Illustrated
Free

We live in a world of sports talk radio, hours of blabbermouth sports TV shows, and all manner of blogs and Web sites filled with news coverage, statistics, and prognostication. And oh, yes, there's also the games on television, radio, and the Web. But for more than half a century, *Sports Illustrated* has been the publication of record for sports fans. It came out once a week, and the articles offered a similar though slightly more casual version of the sort of coverage that appeared in its corporate cousin, *TIME* magazine.

It includes shortened versions of the think pieces and columns that run in the magazine along with a sampling of photos. And it blends in some up-to-the-second information: scores of major sporting events as they occur, updated statistics and standings for leagues, and breaking news in the world of sports.

You can personalize your front page, and you can choose whether the app stays active in the background, grabbing scores and headlines from the Web; the alternative is for the app to update itself only when you open it up on your BlackBerry.

It's also free — at least at the start. It is unclear whether the app will attempt to make money by selling ads or by charging subscription fees. But like the magazine it springs from, it's a class act.

How to get it
Available from BlackBerry App World. Sports Illustrated. Price: Free.

TIME
Free

The magazine that pioneered the concept of the news weekly in 1923 has been through many changes in its nine decades, and has now arrived in a downsized form on the small screen of the BlackBerry. Over the years, *TIME* grew into a very influential publication, but its importance was diminished by the arrival of television and, more recently, by the Internet. Each served to make the magazine's news seem outdated well before it arrived on the newsstand or in your mailbox.

In some ways, the mobile version of *TIME* is the magazine reborn. It also offers the chance to browse through color photos and special sections, including weekly lists of things you need to know. It includes many of the news articles, analysis pieces, and columns from the print version and it also adds current headlines, updates, and blogs.

When you add this app to your phone, you'll receive updates automatically, and you can read them even when you are not communicating with the Web. Even better, the BlackBerry app is free. *TIME* does have room for some ads on its small pages and there may someday be other income streams for the publication; for the moment, though, this app plants the *TIME* flag on the smartphone. And it has a bit of style: the hallmark red border of the print magazine lives on as an accent above the mobile version's front page.

How to get it

Available through BlackBerry App World or from the developer, Time, Inc. To download directly, open the Web browser on your BlackBerry and enter **http://app.time.com**. Price: Free.

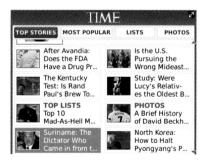

6 Finance

 ATM Hunter
Free

Sometimes you've just got to go to a real bank — or at least to an ATM — to deposit a paper check or get some cash for those few places where you are unable to pay for something with plastic. ATM Hunter, offered as a free app by MasterCard, is aptly named: it finds the nearest electronic banking center, tells you some details about its location and services, and then presents a map so you can go hunt it down.

Even better: if your BlackBerry has GPS circuitry built in it can determine your location automatically and then display an active map or a set of step-by-step instructions that will get you from here to there. What is an active map? It's a display that follows you as you move and changes its orientation and directional arrow as needed. If you are on foot, it will get you there block by block; if you are in a car, it is similar to the display of a dedicated GPS unit.

As I tested this app, I realized that a clever BlackBerry user could use it as a free GPS router: just select an ATM or banking center that is near where you want to end up and then wave at the bank as you head for your actual destination.

If your BlackBerry does not have GPS functionality or access, you can tell the app your current address and let it consult its database to find ATMs that are nearby. You'll still get instructions from here to there, but they won't be interactive. And you can also search for ATMs by airport. Just enter the name of the particular purgatory in which you are trapped and it will tell you where to look. It will also display a map of the airport.

There are some limitations. Since this app is supplied by MasterCard, in theory it will only show banks or ATMs that accept that particular brand of plastic. However, Visa and other credit and debit cards usually are associated with one or another large network of machines, which blurs the distinction between the two brands.

Amongst the details displayed by the list of ATMs is the name of the bank or the private network it uses, whether the location is open all the time, and whether it is handicapped-accessible. There is also a filter that purports to tell you if the provider does not charge an access fee, but in my tests that feature did not appear to be working.

I like this little tool for what it does, and I am also excited about the fact that live GPS features are included as a free and fully integrated function. Next up: fully intelligent pizza hunters, Chinese food explorers, and parking spot locators.

Best features

Free active GPS location sensing and turn-by-turn directions displayed on a map and in a list of instructions.

Worst features

You're on your own learning how to use the app; there are no help screens. It's also large, occupying about 1.7MB of device memory.

How to get it

Available from BlackBerry App World. Developer: MasterCard. Price: Free.

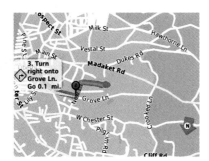

Mobile Checkbook
$ US

In some ways, Mobile Checkbook is way behind the curve. How many checks do you write per day, and how often do you write them while you are away from your desk or study? This app is intended to serve as a quick and simple recording device on your BlackBerry for checks you write and deposits you make while out and about. It is very attractively designed and works quite well. In my case, the answers to the questions I posed are zero and none. I do almost all of my checking from the keyboard of my desktop computer or occasionally from the app on my smartphone provided by my bank.

But I do use a debit and credit card all the time, and sometimes I pay cash. And it would be nice to be able to keep track of my expenditures while I travel. And so I have taken Mobile Checkbook for BlackBerry and made it my own. The app comes equipped with a savings and checking category.

I created three accounts that match my style:

✔ Credit cards

✔ Debit cards

✔ Cash expenditures

mobilecheckbook	Transaction List
Available Balance $522.05	
8/16 -$2200.00 Invest the profits	
8/16 -$14.50 Piece-a-Pizza	
8/16 +$2333.34 Receipts from lemonade stand	
8/15 -$112.56 Foggy Island Farms	
8/14 -$24.46 Stop & Hop	
8/2 +$540.23 Opening balance	

The app allows an unlimited number of bank accounts; I just repurposed their categories. Now I can enter transactions as I make them or hold on to receipts and punch them in at the end of the day: date, amount, business name, and a notes field to hold any comments I care to make. Each account can be reconciled when statements from banks or credit card companies arrive.

And every week or so, I ask Mobile Checkbook to export its listings of transactions by e-mail to one of my accounts. I can choose between two formats:

- ✔ XLS, which is used by most spreadsheet programs including Microsoft Excel.

- ✔ QIF, which is used by nearly all personal accounting programs like Quicken.

The app also allows you to create accounts in a variety of currencies, including the U.S. dollar, the British pound, the euro, krona, and the India rupee. With that ability, I can repurpose the app once again, using Mobile Checkbook as an expense tracker when I travel internationally.

This is strictly an electronic recorder of transactions, though. There is no way to sort your entries based on the name of the payee or the type of expenditure. However, you could do that once an exported file arrives on your personal computer and you open it within a spread-sheet or finance program. Yes, repurposing the data.

Best features

The ability (whether its designers intended this or not) for users to repurpose this tool to meet their own needs.

Worst features

There is no way to sort entries based on categories like rent, gas, or insurance. The e-mail facility does not tap into the built-in contacts list of the BlackBerry; you'll have to enter addresses manually.

How to get it

Available from BlackBerry App World or from third-party sources like Crackberry. Mobatech LLC. www.mobatech.com. Price: $4.99.

Morningstar Mobile
Free

Everyone's got to make a buck some way. Some financial tools are put forth by brokerage companies that hope to make a profit by enticing you to use their services to buy or sell shares or other forms of investments. Others are offered by information aggregators (like Yahoo!) that intend to boost their earnings by selling advertising.

And then there are sites like Morningstar that have more than one source of income. The basic Web site, at www.morningstar.com, is free to users but carries advertisements as well as enticements to upgrade to premium services that include analyses of your investment portfolio and advanced tools to assist you in buying and selling investment vehicles.

I mention the Web site because that is where you need to begin your use of Morningstar. You register for an account there and set up a portfolio or watch list (or both) that includes stocks, mutual funds, and certain other types of investments. In your portfolio you can list the purchase date and price for shares, which can help you in tax decisions when it comes time to calculate a cost basis for investments.

You can perform research on the Web site and consult news about companies and funds in which you have made investments. Once you have completed the creation of your lists, you then download and install Morningstar Mobile for BlackBerry.

This free app (which uses the same login and password you set up on the Web) allows you to sync to the same portfolios and watch lists. You can view performance charts and access basic Morningstar analysis, including its rating for the investment.

			11:17 AI↗
Portfolio	Related News		
Total Value		**Total Day Change**	
$715,052.57		0.10%	
Ticker	Last Price	%Price Change	$Price ▲Change
KFT	29.46	-0.14	-0.04
BMLPRQ	25.59	-0.04	-0.01
NECLX	12.00	0.00	0.00
ECGOX	7.60	0.13	0.01
FDBCX	9.24	0.22	0.02 ▾

There's a calculation of the day's total value for the portfolio and the overall percent gain or loss in the current session. You can choose to have the app automatically update prices or only when it is opened or the refresh menu item chosen. The app can also be set to use Wi-Fi when available

If you are already working with an investment advisor, the free app may be sufficient for your purposes; it gives you quick access to a report on the performance of your investments at any time. But if you are managing your own investments (or if you want a second, independent analysis of your holdings), you may want to consider upgrading to premium services.

Among the advanced tools is Instant X-Ray, which looks at your asset allocation and tells you how well it fits your investment style including tolerance for risk. It also looks for overlaps and conflicts amongst mutual funds. And it shows you the percentage of your investments in various sectors of the economy: for example, what portion of your portfolio is allocated to services or manufacturing and how that compares to the S&P 500's allocation.

Best features

This is a tool that goes beyond the basics for the well-informed investor. And because it is not linked to a brokerage, users can be reasonably comfortable about storing some of their personal financial information on the Web site; a strong password will complete the wall around your data.

Worst features

The lure to purchase the premium edition is pretty strong; its features are listed on many screens but you can't get the results without paying the admission fee.

How to get it

Available from BlackBerry App World and from the developer. Morningstar. http://mobileapps.morningstar.com/mobile2/bb.aspx. Price: Free for basic service; as much as $179 per year for a premium subscription.

Personal Assistant
Free

I start out with a confession: there is no way, off the top of my head, I could remember all of my credit card and banking accounts, utility, insurance, association memberships, and other financial obligations.

I'm very happy with the current trend with banks and other institutions sending bills and accepting payment online. And though I do check all statements, I also have instructed most of them to make automatic withdrawals from my banking account when payments are due so that I never have to worry about late fees. But everything is scattered about in 12 or 30 different Web sites. I have no way to get the big picture: how much do I owe this month?

That is where Personal Assistant promises to help, and it delivers pretty well. If you trust it with your login names and passwords it will keep in touch with all of the companies where you have accounts, posting the current balance due. It will remind you when payments are due — by on-screen message and by adding notations to the BlackBerry calendar. The app (known as Pageonce on the Web and other smartphones) can also pass along alerts from the companies with which you do business: overdue notices, changes to interest rates, and certain special offers.

The product is available in a free edition which is limited in its scope, or in a premium version that permits an unlimited number of accounts, strips away advertising banners, and adds other features.

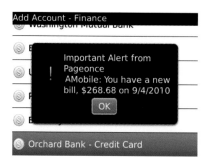

You can turn on alerts that will come from the company's Web site to your BlackBerry to remind you to pay a bill or take other actions.

The makers of the app promise that your passwords and account information will remain private and protected from intrusion. At this point, I am not aware of any breaches of that trust. But users of this app and similar ones — as well as online access to credit cards and bank accounts — should be vigilant in guarding against unauthorized access.

And if you put your trust in this app, it can also serve as a way for you to quickly monitor all of your accounts for fraud. If one of your credit card accounts suddenly starts zooming toward its limit with purchases of expensive shoes in Rome . . . and you are sitting in your den in Chicago . . . you can act immediately to notify the card company and protect yourself.

The inclusion of airline flight status in the premium version of the app hints at what may be the future of products like this. Just as the BlackBerry has thrived by bringing together in one device a number of once-separate gizmos (cellphone, personal data assistant, GPS, digital camera, video camera) so, too, we can expect to see apps that truly become personal assistants.

Need an airline, hotel, and car reservation? An assistant can do that. Then you need to pay for those services. Here, I've got your credit card accounts right here. And then the bill comes due. Want me to pay for that now? I'm just speculating here, you understand . . . but that's the direction I expect apps to take: moving from small individual services to an all-in-one personal servant.

How to get it

Available through BlackBerry App World or from the developer. Pageonce. www.pageonce.com or m.pageonce.com. Price: Free for limited version; $6.99 for premium version.

Car Loan Calculator
$ US

After you've agreed on a car price, for many buyers the next headache involves financing. And here Car Loan Calculator can put the numbers in the palm of your hand. Enter the amount that will be financed, the number of months for the loan, and the interest rate and click Calculate. You'll have your own numbers: the monthly payments and the total amount of money you will have to pay over the full term of the loan.

That's good enough, but you can also compare one interest rate against another. Obviously, a 4 percent interest rate is better than a 5 percent rate, but exactly how much money are we talking about across four years? You can also look at the same information as a color pie chart that shows you how much of your money will go for the principal and how much for the interest over the course of time.

And one other interesting screen allows you to see the real cost difference between cars that have higher or lower miles per gallon ratings. In one example I tried, based on driving an average of 300 miles per week (about 15,000 miles per year) a car that gets 27 mpg might cost about $900 less to operate per year than one that delivers only 19 mpg.

It would also be very valuable to be able to compare two loans of differing interest rates and number of months.

How to get it
Available from third-party sites such as Crackberry and the developer. Jengun. www.jengun.com. Price: $3.99.

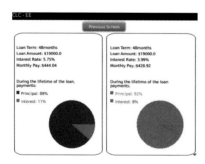

ING Direct
Free

While Bank of America Mobile is the online or smartphone extension of a bricks-and-mortar bank, ING Direct is a virtual bank that has no retail offices. Its entire business plan is based on electronic transactions: direct deposits, withdrawals, and transfers. ING Direct is an offshoot of a "real" bank in the Netherlands, but in the United States as well as Canada, the United Kingdom, western Europe, and Australia it does its business with computer bits and telephone nibbles.

Like a number of other BlackBerry apps involving finances and investments, this product serves as a quick and easy window into the full listings and functions of a Web site. You set up your account on the Internet and then use the same customer ID and password on the BlackBerry to perform basic functions and make use of predefined transfers or payments.

It offers a true BlackBerry app, with simple-to-read and easy-to-use screens that allow you to transfer money between accounts, pay bills, and P2P direct deposits into any other person's bank account within or outside of the ING virtual world.

How to get it

Available through BlackBerry App World or directly from the ING Direct Web site you use for online banking. Price: Free.

PayPal
Free

It's not a bank any more than its corporate parent eBay is a store. PayPal is an e-commerce intermediary that allows just about anyone to pay just about anyone else for goods or services rendered. The company arose as a way to meet the needs of individual sellers on eBay to accept payment from buyers, an alternative to checks and money orders. As a buyer you can pay for something with a credit card or an electronic transfer from your checking account; the proceeds are transmitted (minus a service charge) to the seller.

Just as eBay became a multibillion dollar success without ever having to actually warehouse, market, or ship any actual products so too has PayPal thrived entirely as a service. PayPal has now grown to the point where it handles transactions for all sorts of clients (not just within eBay), and its annual volume exceeds that of the sales at eBay. As such it exists in most parts of the globe in a netherworld somewhere between a financial service and a bank. In some countries outside of the United States it also operates as an actual bank.

An account with the company is free, and once established you can receive money from anyone you deal with. As with the other financial institutions in this section, all of the detailed work is accomplished at an online Web site accessed from a computer; once that has been established you can use the PayPal app on your BlackBerry to send or receive money.

How to get it

Available through BlackBerry App World or directly from PayPal.com. Price: Free.

Calculate 4-in-1
$ US

Okay, so there are four of us out to dinner. We ordered modestly and shared a bottle of relatively inexpensive wine. The bill came to $132.60 and that includes 8 percent sales tax. We feel a bit magnanimous. The waitress was cute and she worked really hard, especially after you-know-who sent back the vegetables because she thought they were undercooked. So we want to bump up the tip to 17 percent.

Quick: How much do each of us owe? And of course, we don't want to include the sales tax in our math. Easy as pie: $38.33, according to Calculate 4-in-1.

This is a simple and straightforward specialized calculator for four important (though unequal) tasks in life:

- Determining a tip.
- Figuring out mortgage payments and amortization.
- Checking a car loan payment.
- Toting up how much money we can earn in compound interest in a CD or savings account.

Answer the questions, click the Calculate button, and read off the numbers. It's not going to impress people at a party, but it's useful and simple.

How to get it

Available from third-party sites such as Crackberry and the developer. Jengun. www.jengun.com. Price: $3.99.

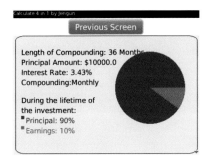

MobyQuote
Free

High finance can bring high anxiety — for both the customer and the sales rep. MobyQuote is a straight-to-the-point specialized financial calculator aimed at lenders who need to quickly calculate — and adjust when necessary — terms for a lease or loan.

This is the sort of app that will seem simple and easy to someone who has to wrestle with loan terms regularly. If that's not your area of specialty or need, this power tool may be way too focused for you; you'll want a more full-featured program that runs on a laptop or desktop.

In a nutshell, it works like this: enter the type of yield (monthly or annual) you need to achieve and then enter the sale price. Other fields you can work with include administrative fees and commissions. You can enter a term (number of months) and let the app work out the monthly payment or you can enter the monthly payment and let it tell you how long the loan will run or how much the borrower can be advanced.

Each field is adjustable. If it takes a reduction in the interest rate to make a deal work, that can be changed and the numbers reworked. Longer term for lower payment? No problem. Add a balloon at the end? Done.

This app does the basic work. The developer also sells an advanced version on a subscription basis that uploads the details from a loan calculation into your company's accounting or lending forms.

How to get it

BlackBerry App World or from the developer. Mobile Productivity. www.mobyquote.com. Price: Free.

```
                 $1117.78
Reference
  BlackBerry Orchards
Yield Basis
    Monthly Nominal
Yield
              2.9998
Sale Price
            52000
```

MyStocks
$ US

In the category of *stuff* my dad says, there was this bit of critical advice about the stock market: "They don't ring a bell at the top." It's advice I have more or less followed all my life. If I buy a stock or a mutual fund and I think it is overpriced in the market, I usually sell it, count my profits, and don't agonize (too much) if it continues to rise. Which brings me to MyStocks, a very simple tool to track just one thing: the price of shares of stock or mutual funds.

You enter the stock symbol in a list and the app displays its current price, including any rises or falls during the current day. If you click the BlackBerry Menu key, you can ask the app to give you details on the stock: the bid and ask price, the previous close, the 52-week range. You can also display from 3 to 20 months of prices, and jump to www. Yahoo.com for a full page of information about the company's financials and operations.

Three things it won't do: keep track of your actual portfolio with number of shares and current value, allow you to buy or sell, or ring a bell at the top. There are more sophisticated and expensive programs that allow you to do two out of three of those tasks. MyStocks is instead just a humble market ticker in your pocket.

How to get it
Available from third-party sites such as Crackberry. Developer: Toysoft Development, Inc. Price: $2.99.

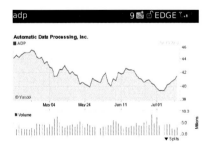

Bank of America Mobile
Free

The fact is that this app is actually just a shortcut that goes onto the Internet to a mobile version of the Bank of America online site; it's not fully optimized for the BlackBerry. It does, though, seem to be as secure as any online transactions. It includes the ability to check the balance and transactions of your accounts, transfer money between accounts, and pay any bills you have previously set up. It is intended to be your quick-and-easy companion while you are away from your home or office. Before you can use this app on your BlackBerry you need to set up an online account from a computer.

The sign-on screen offers to let you store the name of your account so that it appears each time you choose the app; I prefer not to take that risk, at least until they come up with an iris scan or a fingerprint reader for the BlackBerry.

You're notified if the bank does not recognize the phone you are using as one that has accessed the account before. This is a second level of security; you can choose to allow the bank to put a cookie (an identifier) on your phone or you can answer one of the security questions you had previously set up. The app also offers to tell you the nearest branch or ATM machine based on your zip code or an address you enter.

One of the advantages of using an app like Bank of America Mobile on your BlackBerry device is that your transaction is not using someone else's connection to the Internet.

How to get it
Available through BlackBerry App World or directly from the Bank of America Web site you use for online banking. Price: Free.

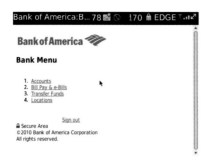

Y! Finance
Free

There's no escaping the ups and downs of the stock market. And with apps like Y! Finance, there's no way to avoid the temptation to check in on your investment portfolio all through the day and into the night. Y! Finance is a window into the full Web page of Yahoo! Finance, which includes a nearly full range of investment tracking and research options. On the Web site you can enter many of the details of your financial holdings: purchase dates, prices, sales, and other elements.

Both Y! Finance and the Yahoo! Finance Web site (at http://finance. yahoo.com) are free, each supported by advertising — mostly by companies trying to sell you additional investment vehicles. It is possible to ignore the commercials and troll through the articles and columns on the Web site for valuable information.

All of the heavy lifting when setting up your portfolio details takes place on your personal computer. The BlackBerry app amounts to a personalized ticker (delayed 15 minutes behind the actual markets). You can expand an individual stock you are monitoring to read a secondary page that tells you the day's trading range for a particular stock, its 52-week range, and its total market capitalization. You can also see an equity's estimated earnings per share and its price-to-earnings ratio. If there is any news that is directly related to that company or to one of its competitors it is also displayed.

If you're looking for a more robust portfolio tracker that will reside on your BlackBerry, you'll have to find one from a brokerage or financial service (and probably provided to established customers).

How to get it
Available from the developer. Yahoo! http://mobile.yahoo.com/ finance. Price: Free.

❾*!* Finance	Portfolio CS		
ADP	39.79	-0.21	-0.53% ⬇
BMY	26.32	-0.01	-0.04% ⬇
CLX	64.31	-0.21	-0.33% ⬇
DUK	17.01	-0.09	-0.53% ⬇
ED	47.55	-0.40	-0.83% ⬇
EMR	48.23	-0.15	-0.31% ⬇
EWS	12.00	+0.10	+0.84% ⬆
EXC	41.37	+0.12	+0.29% ⬆
FTR	7.60	+0.00	+0.00% —
GIM	10.39	-0.02	-0.19% ⬇

7 Calendars and Timers

Top Apps

- Antair RE:Mind
- Dilbert Calendar
- The New Yorker Calendar
- LaterDude Pro
- SBSH Calendar Pro

- SBSH Historia
- Hourglass
- My List
- StickyNote
- SwooshAlarm

Antair RE:Mind
$$ US

Just what I need: an electronic nudge to remind me to make a phone call, send an e-mail, or do something at a particular time. Actually, it's exactly what I need — especially when I am away from my office and relying on my BlackBerry as my link to home and office. This app bridges the gap between your e-mail, phone log, or tasks list and your calendar and alarm clock.

You can use this tool as part of your regular BlackBerry e-mail inbox trolling.

- ✔ Enlist RE:Mind as your personal secretary to prod you to action at a particular time when you come across a message that you want to respond to by mail or phone.

- ✔ Assign a reminder to a missed phone call, choosing the best time for a response.

- ✔ Schedule a wake-up message when there's a task to be done: a calendar appointment, a job you need to do at a particular time, an app that needs to be run.

You can reply to e-mail and return phone calls directly from the reminder without having to look up addresses or phone numbers. This feature and certain other advanced functions will only work on current BlackBerry models. Be sure to check requirements before purchasing this or any other app.

E-Mail follow-up reminders include full contact information and a summary of the original message. Phone call follow-ups include a call-back number and any available caller-ID information.

You can instruct Antair RE:Mind to notify you via sßcreen pop-up, e-mail reminder, or both. And you can add notes to any e-mail, phonecall, or personal reminder. For example, a reminder to attend a meeting can include driving instructions and details of your assigned duties. There is no limit to the number of reminders you can set for yourself. The main screen of RE:Mind allows you to see all pending reminders and you can edit them or reschedule as necessary.

Antair RE:Mind is a product that fits the BlackBerry mold very well. It is well designed and useful. You may not want to show it off to your friends at a cocktail party, but it will help you arrive on time to the party and keep track of the business prospects and professional opportunities who arise. I'll take that over bells and whistles any time.

Best features

This is another component in the very polished series of productivity tools from Antair. It performs as advertised with a minimum of fuss and bother.

Worst features

You'll need to upgrade to a paid license to have more than three nudges waiting to pounce.

How to get it

Available from BlackBerry App World and from third-party sites such as Crackberry. Antair. www.antair.com. Price: $9.99.

Dilbert Calendar
$ US

Attention cubicle dwellers. Hello to culturally and politically hip Gothamites and those who empathize from a distance. We have your calendars. First the cubicle cure. Since 1989, a square-headed guy by the name of Dilbert has brought a bit of subversive sunshine into windowless places of business everywhere. It's a world of clueless bosses, downtrodden and misdirected minions, and a keen eye on the realities of life in The Office, decades before the much less clever television series of the same name appeared.

The Dilbert Calendar delivers a daily animated Dilbert cartoon to your BlackBerry, integrated to your device's built-in calendar. So you can both amuse yourself and become depressed as you survey your day of disorganized meetings, pointless conference calls, and doomed-before-they-start product launches.

Be careful of high bills if you roam outside your home area.

Best features
Laugh out loud funny, if your boss doesn't object.

Worst features
Beware of data charges. And bosses with no sense of humor.

How to get it
Available from BlackBerry App World. Metranome, Inc. Price: Free trial, then subscriptions by the month, half year, or year. Prices range from 99 cents to $9.99 for a full year.

The New Yorker Calendar
$ US

At another point on the circle of modern life are the cartoons of the celebrated magazine *The New Yorker*. Sometimes sophisticated, sometimes silly, often highly topical but occasionally so arcane that it takes a higher degree in English Lit to understand.

Among the most famous of cartoons from the magazine was one that defined the Internet all the way back in 1993: Peter Steiner drew two dogs sitting at a computer and added the caption, "On the Internet, no one knows you're a dog."

The New Yorker Calendar, distributed by the same company as its Dilbert cousin, works the same way: one cartoon or short video each day along with a connection to your BlackBerry's calendar for appointments.

The calendar is offered free but the subscription is only valid for a few days. You should also be aware that the app uses the datastream to download each day's amusement; be careful of high bills if you roam outside your home area.

Best features
Laughter is the best medicine.

Worst features
Beware of data charges.

How to get it
Available from BlackBerry App World. Metranome, Inc. Price: Free trial, then subscriptions by the month, half year, or year. Prices range from 99 cents to $9.99 for a full year.

LaterDude Pro
$ US

"Hey dude (or dudette, if you prefer)! Cut me some slack. I'm busy right now, but I'll get back to you. Later, dude." That encapsulates the purpose and the origin of the name for this simple but valuable app. LaterDude Pro (and its earlier and less capable LaterDude version) are a quick and easy way to remind yourself to get something done: reply to an e-mail, phone someone whose call you missed, answer an SMS text, or be somewhere and do something at a time specific.

Once downloaded and installed, the app insinuates itself into the BlackBerry operating system and appears in most menus. For example, when you open your e-mail folder you can highlight a message, click the Menu key, and instruct LaterDude to remind you to respond at a particular time. Or you can read the message and respond to it and then ask LaterDude to remind you to follow up in a week or to perform a particular task in half an hour.

The reminders can extend to creating a new event in the BlackBerry calendar. You can also go into the phone's call log, address book, or e-mail and SMS folder and ask LaterDude to fill out the fields of a reminder from the information it finds there: name, phone number, e-mail address, BlackBerry PIN, and other details. And you can add to the entry any notes; for example: "Remove all photos of Nancy before she comes over to the house, dude."

The automated entries can be edited and refined from the keyboard of your phone. Once the entry is to your satisfaction, click Save and the event gets added to the calendar.

And the app includes an unusually fulsome set of customization options. When you create a reminder from an e-mail message, LaterDude Pro can save the whole body of the e-mail to the notes field; this brings the e-mail into your calendar for quick reference. You can also decide whether to automatically use the e-mail message's subject as the subject of a new calendar or task event or whether to add your own new topic.

You can instruct the app where to place the cursor when you first call upon LaterDude: at Meet, Call, Contact, SMS, or E-mail. This is an example of a programmer allowing the user to control the behavior of the app, rather than the other way around. And you can set the standard length of a calendar event. The default is ten minutes, but you can adjust the app so that it knows your patterns and preferences. Finally, you can add your own keyword to the display of options shown on the menu. You might want to add "Hide" or "Move Out of Town" or another action.

The app is available in a trial version that limits the number of reminders or the time period before they become active; the trial version can be upgraded to full features with the purchase of a registration key.

Best features

Clever idea, nicely implemented. And the author has applied a steady stream of updates and improvements to the original app, responding to suggestions from users.

Worst features

None, really, except that if you procrastinate people may start calling you the LaterDude guy.

How to get it

Available from third-party sites such as Crackberry and the developer. Fabian. www.mobileutil.com. Price: $2.95.

SBSH Calendar Pro
$$ US

One way to judge the importance (or at least the complexity of life) of a person is to steal a look at their calendar. If it's blank, there's either not a whole lot going on or they have not made use of one of the most valuable features of their BlackBerry: its built-in calendar and appointment book. If it's cluttered and disorganized, they may be busy but they're not pros.

This is the sort of program that you will be looking to install in the BlackBerry PlayBook, the tablet computer introduced by RIM in 2011. This sort of integrated app will be able to reach into your BlackBerry phone's calendar database and make the information it finds there work with your scheduling, presentation, travel management, and other software on the PlayBook. A task that comes in by e-mail on the phone can be synchronized with the calendar and then used to extract data from other programs — all in the palm of your hand.

We start with the fact that every BlackBerry has a perfectly capable calendar that is part of the operating system. Most people use it quite happily. But those of us who are often on the run — and who use our BlackBerry devices as an extension of our personal computers — want more. We want a time-management system. That's what Calendar Pro delivers.

Calendar Pro is an extension or an enhancement to the BlackBerry's built-in calendar database. In addition to keeping the BB calendar and Calendar Pro current with each other, this also extends to any synchronization you do from your BlackBerry to any calendar software you maintain on your personal computer and sync to your phone. It's all automatic, too.

📅 Wed September 1, 2010, week 35

| 7 | 8 | 9 | 10 | 11 | 12 | 1 | 2 | 3 | 4 | 5 | 6 | 7 |

12:00AM-1:00AM

5:00AM-6:00AM
Arrival London. BA112 JFK to LHR 1...
6:20AM-6:20AM
Car service LHR to Southampton.... ⚠
7:20AM-8:20AM
Hilton Southampton. Confirm 512... ⚠
10:00AM-11:00AM
Dinner with Lord Mayor, chambers....
6:00PM-9:00PM

And although Calendar Pro does not offer a way to print a schedule or e-mail it to someone else — features that would be welcome — you can accomplish that by syncing your phone to the calendar on your personal computer.

The calendar integrates appointments and tasks or to-do lists. You can make any item private or public. You can categorize your schedule in the way that works best for you.

When you add an appointment you'll go to a screen with five tabs. The screen for tasks is the same, without the Attendees tab. When you switch from a daily view to a full week, vertical bars show the agenda. Each colored box represents an appointment and empty grids indicate free hours where you can schedule new meetings. And as you move the pointer from box to box, a preview pane at the bottom expands to show details.

All of the items you enter in Calendar Pro are searchable within the app: appointments, meetings, and tasks.

Best features

All of Calendar Pro's features are integrated with the built-in calendar that comes with the BlackBerry. Make a change in one and it is reflected in the other; any other app you use that insinuates itself into the BlackBerry will mesh perfectly.

Worst features

Not the best at dealing with scheduled events like airplane flights that begin in one time zone and end in another; it gets a bit confused and so will you, until you make manual adjustments.

How to get it

Available from BlackBerry App World and from third-party sites such as Crackberry. SBSH Mobile Software. www.sbsh.net. Price: $5.95–$14.95.

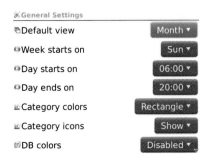

SBSH Historia
$ US

Someday when I pen my masterpiece, I'm going to need to consult my diary. When exactly did I receive that call from my inside source at the Vatican, the one who told me who to call at the CIA for the number of the guy who's got the Holy Grail in a safe hidden behind the stolen Rembrandt in his basement? Why, I've got it all here in my Historia call log. It forgets *nothing*.

Historia is a highly specialized call-logging app. When you give it permission, it idles quietly in the background waiting for you to make or receive a call using your BlackBerry. When the moment arrives, it springs into action and makes a record of as much detail as is available: incoming or outgoing, the number dialed or that called you, the caller ID or the contact information from your address book, and the date and time the call began and ended.

And then it puts that information in two places. It automatically makes an entry in your BlackBerry calendar with all of the data, and it also stores the record in a CSV file that you can export to a personal computer and open in a spreadsheet or database program.

> 15185550101
>
> 📧 Incoming Call
> ⏰ 7/26/10, 6:02 PM
> ⏱ 00:23
> 📵 Do not accept
> 📶 Not Available

For some of us, this is a great way to keep track of what we're doing and who we're talking to from our BlackBerry device. But for other users, that's going to result in a whole lot of information cluttering up the calendar. If that's you, limit the logging to specific numbers by entering them ahead of time to a list maintained by the app. Or tell Historia to log only incoming or only outgoing calls.

You can also open up your calendar and add notes about the subject of the conversation, enter any follow-up tasks, and even send a copy of the calendar notation by e-mail or SMS to yourself, to the person you spoke with, or to another address.

Now there is one important caveat here for those of you who might be thinking that this app will serve in some way as a legal document to prove that you made or received a call at a particular time or even that a particular phone number was involved: The records that are created in the BlackBerry calendar are fully editable. You can change the number that is listed, change the time the call began or ended, and otherwise tamper with the evidence.

This app is more like an automatic notation in a notebook. You can use it for your own purposes but if someone wanted to challenge its accuracy, you'd have to go one step beyond: contact your cellphone provider and obtain a copy of the call records they maintain. (They're pretty good at it, after all: they send you a bill each month for your BlackBerry use.)

Best features

Set it and forget it. It does its thing automatically in the background.

Worst features

If you make or receive a lot of calls, you're going to want to either filter the numbers that are recorded to the calendar or go in and edit the calendar regularly.

How to get it

Available from BlackBerry App World and from third-party sites such as Crackberry. SBSH Mobile Software. www.sbsh.net/products/BlackBerry/historia. Price: $3.99.

All calls	
Home This Phone	00:24
Capture Screen...	7/28/10, 9:59 AM
Details	00:00
Call	7/28/10, 8:40 AM
SMS	
Save to Contacts Inc.	00:05
Copy	7/26/10, 6:02 PM
Filter	00:23
Delete	
Filter by Incoming	7/25/10, 12:10 PM
Filter by Outgoing	00:34

Hourglass
$ US

How's this for the ultimate in revisionist thinking (something of which Luddites would surely approve)? The Hourglass app takes your technological marvel — the handheld BlackBerry that has more computing power than the astronauts had when they landed on the moon — and turns back the hands of time to put an hourglass on the screen.

It's a beautiful hourglass, handsomely rendered. And it includes very few minor adjustments, but it is just a picture of a glass device with sand that runs from the upper chamber to the lower chamber. You can set the hourglass timer to several timing ranges, from a few minutes up to an hour. You can pause the trickle of sand by pressing the spacebar. And you can change the theme for the background or the color of the sand. That's it, folks.

On the BlackBerry Bold 9700 used as this book's test device, the hourglass displayed sideways across the horizontal screen. It's not a big deal; you just turn the device 90 degrees and sit and stare at the movement of sand.

I'm looking forward to the next board of directors' meeting for my company. I fully intend to set up my electronic hourglass on a stand and turn it on before calling the session to order.

How to get it

Available from BlackBerry App World and from third-party sites such as Crackberry. BB Soft. http://foryourblackberry.com. Price: $1.99.

My List
$ US

I've got so many lists of things that need to be done: must-dos for today, honey-dos from my wife, shopping lists, books I want to read, music I want to download, and packing reminders for upcoming trips. What I need is a list of lists, and then some sort of way to track items that are completed and those that are yet to be done. That's what the app My List does. (The app is also known as Things on some sites.)

My List comes with a set of predefined categories, including daily and weekend, shopping, house ideas, books, music, and various celebrations. You can create others of your own, applying any of more than 30 icons to help you distinguish one from another. Within each category you then create items.

Once you accomplish a particular task or purchase an item, you can check it off on your list but leave the category still in place. Or you can delete the item or the category once a complete list has been fulfilled.

The concept for this app is about as simple as a set of index cards taped to the refrigerator or thumb-tacked to a corkboard. But in simplicity there is hope of actually accomplishing something.

How to get it

Available from BlackBerry App World and from third-party sources such as Crackberry. Price: $3.99.

StickyNote
$ US

Note to self: invent something so simple but so useful that it will sell billions of copies. If only. A chemist invented a sticky-but-not-permanent Post-it glue and years later another employee swabbed some on the back of a piece of paper and changed the world.

The BlackBerry has become a portable extension of our life, holding our personal and business information and our connection to the outside world. I consult the calendar on my phone and the e-mail inbox dozens of times during the day. But I still need reminders now and again.

Choice one: attach a small Post-it to the phone screen. Better choice: use a reminder app like StickyNote that places a virtual note on the BlackBerry's home screen.

StickyNote is a simple app. Open it, enter some text on a note, and post it on the screen. It stays there until you reopen the app and delete or edit it to include the next reminder. You can adjust the note's location, size, font, background color, or design.

The app also adds a StickyNote item to the menus displayed from the home page, calendar, contact list, and elsewhere. This allows you to easily add or edit the note based on information you are consulting.

How to get it

Available from BlackBerry App World, from third-party sources such as Crackberry, and from the developer. CellAvant. Price: $2.99.

SwooshAlarm
$ US

Nobody particularly loves an alarm clock. It pushes us to get out of bed on mornings when we'd rather sleep in. It reminds us of dentist appointments. Face it: an alarm clock is a professional nudge. That said, SwooshAlarm is a better alarm clock than the one that is included as part of the BlackBerry operating system.

First of all, you can set as many alarms as you'd like with all sorts of customized features. You can set them for a particular day or every day. And you can create world clocks for places you are traveling to or where you otherwise need to know the time.

And plans call for the product to add one more feature — it was in beta testing as this book was prepared — that allows you to set an alarm to go off when you arrive at a specific location. Ask your BlackBerry to check its GPS or its cell tower locator and then ring your chimes (or its own) when you both arrive. Another feature in the works will allow you to substitute a snippet of MP3 music or sound effects for one of the built-in alarm sounds of the BlackBerry.

Swoosh has invented a better alarm clock, and now we'll see if the world will beat a path to its door.

How to get it

Available from BlackBerry App World and from third-party sites such as Crackberry. Swoosh Software. www.swooshsoftware.com. Price: $4.99.

8 Entertainment

Top Apps

- Pandora
- Shazam
- CrazySoft Personality Psychology Pro
- Depth of Field Calculator
- EasyBartender
- Fast Food Calorie Counter
- iSpy Cams for BlackBerry
- Links Scorecard
- Nobex Radio Companion
- Sid Meier's Railroad Tycoon
- Aces Solitaire Pack 2
- Aces Traffic Pack
- Flixster
- Greeting Cards Maker
- Moviefone
- Next Dual Pack
- Nintaii
- Pinball Deluxe
- Round of Applause
- Vorino Fractal Explorer

Pandora
Free

Yes, I am old enough to remember radio; in fact, I remember the days before they were portable; big boxy things with a plug. We had our favorite radio stations, and usually a preferred disk jockey. It might have been someone who either was "hip" enough to introduce us to music we'd never heard before but that suited our personal styles. Or it may have been a DJ who stayed within a very tightly defined category that never tested our boundaries: all-Beatles weekends, Sinatra Sundays, Motown Mondays.

But Pandora has opened another box. Think of it as your personal electronic disk jockey that starts with a few songs or artists you like and then searches out and finds music that is similar or shares certain attributes. (If you like Paul Simon, you'll probably like James Taylor and you may not know how much in common both have with the Everly Brothers and selected songs by Elvis. Or Bob Dylan to Pete Seeger and Woodie Guthrie with side trips to Robert Johnson, Muddy Waters, and the Rolling Stones.)

Pandora is actually a relative old-timer in the world of the Internet, rising out of the Music Genome Project that began in 2000. Over the years a team of musicians and music lovers has been sitting around and listening to recordings old and new, popular and obscure. (What a job! Almost as good as sitting around and playing with BlackBerry apps for a living.)

The experts rate each song for as many as 400 attributes: its musical DNA or genome, if you like. The details include style, instrumentation, rhythm, tempo, harmony, the subject of its lyrics, the type of singer, and the secret sauce that makes a song a hit or a flop (for me, but possibly not for you).

As a user, you get to create and fine-tune your own "stations." You're allowed as many as 100 channels and you can pick just one to play, rotate through them all, or ask the computer to choose pleasing songs at random. Although you are able to pause playback, you cannot rewind or replay a song. There are some other strictures, mostly related to copyright issues, including a limitation on the number of times a particular artist can be played per month. But in theory, you should be hearing enough similar music and musicians to eliminate that as an issue.

Your BlackBerry will display a picture of the album or CD cover. And if somehow Pandora casts a swine amongst the pearls, you can remove it from the mix with a click. The more feedback you provide, the better the electronic DJ gets to understand your ear. But before you do, stop and think: why is this song in the mix? Is there something you're missing? Are there other artists or other genres you should explore? You can ask Pandora why its computers recommended a particular song or artist. You may find an unusual commonality between knowns and unknowns in your musical tastes.

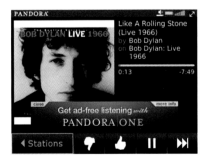

My Pandora mix includes more than a dozen stations that reflect my musical tastes (mostly frozen in the Swinging Sixties). I've got a station called "House of the Rising Sun" that is based around that seminal bluesy song and I enjoy seeing how old and new artists are related to it. The same goes for a station called "Season of the Witch" which branches off the 1966 song by Donovan and has since been covered by dozens of artists including British jazz-blues-rock singer Julie Driscoll when she sang with Brian Auger and his band. And my contemporary stations include one called "Alison Krauss, Dixie Chicks, and Joan Baez," which includes songs by those righteous babes and others of their ilk and of their style.

Pandora on the BlackBerry is free. It is mostly supported by small ads that appear on the screen, although you may not even notice them if your BlackBerry is in your pocket. On your PC or Mac, you can also purchase song downloads as well as concert tickets and other items; that function has not yet arrived on the BlackBerry.

If you have a nice Bluetooth headset, or perhaps a wired or wireless external speaker (I write about these options in Chapter 9 of this book) you can enhance the quality of the playback nicely. In fact, the Jabra Cruiser — one of the devices I mention later — can even rebroadcast Pandora onto your home stereo or the one in your car. However, the quality of signal that comes across on the BlackBerry is always going to be lower than the one that arrives on a broadband cable or DSL Internet connection.

Pandora has slightly tightened "free" to mean that you can listen for 40 hours each calendar month without charge. After then, you have the opportunity to pay for more music. And they also offer Pandora One, which provides higher quality audio and has no limitations on monthly usage; Pandora One is not yet available for mobile devices, though.

Most of the major cellphone providers have no objection to you using Pandora on your BlackBerry, although as I have mentioned you do need to pay attention to the terms of your contract regarding data use per month. If your provider blocks the Pandora app, as a small number do, you may be able to get to it anyway by using the Web browser and using the full Internet version of the program.

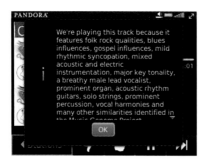

In some ways, Pandora is complementary to Shazam, which I write about in this chapter. Shazam listens to a song you are playing and identifies it. Pandora learns the sort of songs you like to listen to and then seeks to find similar music you may or may not already have on your personal playlist.You knew I had to get around the name of the product, right? Pandora means "all gifted" in Greek. And in Greek mythology she was the first woman, gifted with all sorts of special attributes by the gods. And then — a bit like Eve, I suppose — she got into trouble by opened a jar or a box that she shouldn't have. In doing so, she unleashed a storm of evils upon us all, leaving only Hope inside.

In 2010, Pandora (the music service, that is) had more than 700,000 tracks in its library and some 48 million registered users. That's a whole lot of mostly good music and a lot of hope. Personally, I think Pandora (the legend) and Eve are by now well off the hook for the world's evils.

Best features

Good music, chosen by your personal DJ based on your individual tastes and with very minimal interruption by advertisers.

Worst features

Pandora warns you up front: using streaming radio on your BlackBerry is going to use a lot of data. If you have a truly unlimited data plan, that's no problem. If you pay by the megabyte, though, Pandora is going to open a box of expensive data charges.

How to get it

Available from BlackBerry App World and from third-party sites such as Crackberry. Pandora Media. www.pandora.com/blackberry. Price: Free for basic service; 99 cents for unlimited tunes per month.

Shazam
Free

Yowzah! This is one of those apps where you want to grab a non-techie by the lapels and say, "You've got to see this!" Shazam is a musicologist in your pocket. Turn it on, aim your BlackBerry toward the speakers of your stereo, the background music in a bar, or the fuzzy noise in an elevator, and give it a few seconds to listen and then think.

It's also the ultimate argument settler: is that George Harrison singing "It's been a long time, now I'm coming back home" or is it someone else? Like magic, there on the screen of your BlackBerry — almost without fail — you will see the name of the song, the artist performing it, and the album on which it was released. Want more? How about a biography of the performer, a listing of songs recorded, and access to YouTube and other videos about the singer.

And yes, I won the bet. That was a relatively obscure cover of the Beatles song, performed by Ben Kweller. I couldn't remember the singer's name, but Shazam figured it out. It took two tries to identify a very obscure recording: "Sally Go 'Round the Roses" by Grace Slick and the Great Society, a collector's reissue of recordings she made before that band broke up and Grace broke through to fame as the lead singer of the Jefferson Airplane.

I call this magic, but of course there is technology behind it. Shazam captures a snippet of sound (it's called "tagging" the music) and sends it over the Internet to its computer center. There it compares an acoustic fingerprint of the music you have sent to a huge collection of fingerprints it has on file. Apparently the company is able to identify most songs by comparing a small group of peak intensity frequencies; no matter how complex a song is, it can be encoded at the Shazam end and the little snippet you send matched to it.

When it finds a match — and it almost always does — it sends back a message chock-full of detail to your BlackBerry. Occasionally, if the sound quality is not great or if the music is very obscure, it may take two or three tries before a match is made. And very rarely, the magic doesn't happen; I tried as hard as I could to find obscure music and Shazam was only stumped a few times, and I suspect it was because the music I was playing had not been on the market for many decades.

I set my 300-disc CD carousel on random and let it choose a few tracks. "Muskrat" by Doc Watson with his son Merle: no problem for Shazam. On the information tab there was a substantial biography of the great guitar picker. The discography listed 15 of his albums with a picture of the cover and a track-by-track listing. And I could share my tag by clicking a button to send a Tweet, an SMS text, a BlackBerry PIN call, or an e-mail. The note tells the recipient that you just discovered a new song and suggests they find a copy; you can also add your own comments.

And you can even download a Tag Chart that tells you what the rest of the world, or at least those who are using Shazam, are currently tagging and grooving to. For certain artists and songs — depending on copyrights — you may be able to download the lyrics. And you can also obtain a list of other artists and albums that contain a particular song — by the songwriter or covers by others.

The free version of Shazam has a full set of features, but you'll continu-ally be encouraged to upgrade to a paid subscription to Shazam Encore. Extended features include the Shazam Tag Chart, which gives you a peek at what huge numbers of other users of the app are checking out.

If you know what you're looking for, you can also search through a data-base of eight million songs for any of the following in particular:

- ✔ Lyric
- ✔ Artist
- ✔ Album
- ✔ Track

You can share your tags with friends by sending any of the following:

- ✔ SMS text message
- ✔ E-mail
- ✔ PIN message

When you tag a piece of music, your phone will send a data packet of about 20KB; the snippet of music is not stored on your phone. Then Shazam, once it identifies the music, will send a reponse that includes text and artwork from the cover, totaling about 50KB. That's not a whole lot of data, but unless you have an unlimited data plan you need to be aware that your cellphone provider will charge you for the exchange of bits.

I am also intrigued by other possibilities presented by audio tagging. I can envision your BlackBerry recognizing a voice it hears in a con-versation and then displaying all of the contact information you have stored in the device. It would be a whole lot better than a Hello, My Name Is lapel card.

Best features

It's one of the niftiest pieces of technology out there; if someone asks you what's so great about having a BlackBerry instead of just a dumb old cellphone, make a bet with them that you can identify the next song that plays on the radio or the stereo system.

Worst features

Why do they keep playing "Dancing Queen" in the cocktail lounge?

How to get it

Available from BlackBerry App World and from the developer. Shazam Entertainment Limited. www.shazam.com. Price: Free for basic service; $4.99 for Encore version.

CrazySoft Personality Psychology Pro
$$ US

Is he The One? Is she too perfect for you? Are you playing with a full deck of SIM cards? You might wonder a bit about a vendor of personality tests, CrazySoft Limited, but that's the way it is with this psychologist on a memory chip. There are some 30 different psychological profile "tests" with about 1,000 questions.

Now, for the record, I have included this app in the section about entertainment. This is not the same as seeing a qualified mental health professional if you or someone you know is experiencing difficulties in life.

That said, this is an interesting and fun way to break the ice at a party or a bar or just amongst friends. As many as three people can each set up a profile and then go through a section of the "tests" presented and then compare the results:

✔ Are you highly sociable?

✔ Are you impulsive?

✔ Are you a hypochondriac?

You can even stray a bit further into what may be — for some people — dangerous territory.

✔ What is your level of sexual libido?

✔ Are you sexually permissive?

✔ Where do you stand on the scale of masculinity or femininity?

The questions are ones that would not offend a psychologist or surprise anyone who has ever taken a standardized psychological profile. But the maker of the app does not credit any of the recognized tests.

(In other words, don't expect to be able to translate the results you get into an equivalent score on the widely used MMPI test administered by some businesses, schools, and medical professionals.)

There are some games and entertainments and even some open-ended text questions to pose around the table and see how different people react differently: are their responses compassionate, uncaring, violent, or just plain odd?

There are also questions that seek to elicit a score on such things as racism, religious beliefs, and political positions from libertarian to reactionary. I'd suggest you think twice and maybe three times before taking these tests amongst strangers.

You don't answer questions by moving the trackpad or trackball; instead you enter your response to a question by pressing the appropriate number key on the phone.

Best features

It's an entertaining exercise in pop psychology and in the right circumstances it could help you better understand yourself and your new or longtime friends.

Worst features

As with any psychological test, these questions can be pretty easily defeated by a clever participant who is determined to show a particu

How to get it

Available from BlackBerry App World and from third-party sites such as Crackberry. CrazySoft. www.crazysoft.gr. Price: $6.99.

Depth of Field Calculator
$ US

Speaking of crazy, what is this app doing in a section on entertainment? If you are of a certain kind — a geeky photo fan who remembers how things were before A) digital cameras, B) BlackBerry devices, and C) tiny computers you can hold in your hand — this is the sort of app that can get you excited.

First a definition: "Depth of field" is a term used in optics (lenses) in photography, and although it was first developed for use with film cameras it is still of importance with digital cameras. It is the three-dimension portion of an image that appears acceptably sharp. When a lens focuses on a person or an object at a particular distance it will also be acceptably in focus for a certain distance on either side of what is most in focus. The smaller the f-stop (the aperture or opening of the lens), the greater or wider the depth of field becomes.

Oh yes, there is a another element. The longer the focal length of the lens, the greater the possible depth of field. A wide-angle lens has a much larger or deeper DOF than a telephoto lens. For example, if you focus a telephoto lens on a baseball player standing at home plate, the catcher and umpire just behind him may be a bit fuzzy and the pitcher standing 60 feet away will certainly be out of focus.

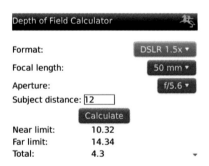

As a photographer, there are times when you might want to have a large depth of field (for example, for a photo of a landscape or of a sporting event or a concert where you want to convey the large size of a place). And there are situations where you might want to have a very limited DOF (in a closeup portrait where you want the subject's face to be sharply imaged but the background falling away to a purposeful blur). As I said, the same principle applies to digital cameras. But as digital cameras have become more and more advanced in their "automatic" features, the special details of things like manually choosing a depth of field have become almost forgotten.

Nearly every digital camera comes with a "zoom" lens that effectively changes the length of the lens along the range from wide angle to telephoto. And many (but not all) digital cameras also have a way to allow you to manually select an aperture or f-stop. Sometimes you cannot directly change the f-stop but you can set the sensor's ISO (speed); the higher the ISO, the smaller the aperture is going to be, which means the greater the depth of field.

So, with all of this sorta-complex background, along comes this very simple but very effective little BlackBerry app. You enter the focal length of the lens, the aperture, and the distance to whatever you want to be in perfect focus. Click Calculate and the screen displays the near limit and the far limit of what will be in acceptable focus.

And then you need to make the same settings on your camera: choose an aperture and select a precise focus point. On some completely point-and-shoot cameras that may be difficult if not impossible; on more advanced cameras you can find the sometimes hidden door to manual control.

Best features

The app can be used with a standard film camera and lens, or make focal length adjustments when matching a standard lens to the small sensor that substitutes for a frame of film on most digital cameras.

Worst features

None really. This is a sharply focused, special tool.

How to get it

Available from BlackBerry App World and from third-party sites such as Crackberry. GLN LLC. www.gln.bz. Price: $2.99.

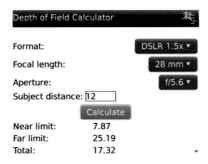

EasyBartender
$ US

"Hey, bud, can you mix me up a Balalaika? You don't know what that is? Here, let me show you the recipe, right here on my BlackBerry." It doesn't matter whether you are sidling up to the bar in a trendy bistro in Silicon Valley or a grungy dive along the railroad tracks in Podunk, this is going to be a great conversation starter. Some conversations may be more enjoyable than others.

The crowd I run with just loves geeky technology. And, on occasion, we enjoy the occasional pre-dinner aperitif. Also an interesting libation with our meal. And then, of course, a post-prandial digestif. In other words, I enjoy a mixed drink from time to time. But I have to admit that this is not one of my areas of expertise. I can mix my own Bloody Mary (actually I prefer the English Mary, which uses gin instead of vodka) and my wife knows how to order (if not make) a decent mojito.

But if you're going to get serious about this, EasyBartender is a very nicely designed and incredibly fulsome app. It includes more than 12,000 drinks: the name, the ingredients, the mixing method, and the proper glass. You can search for drinks by name, by type of alcohol, or by method of mixology. And you can have the recipe with measurements by the shot (in ounces) or by the milliliter.

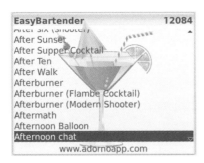

The app shows the signs of a nicely polished piece of software. You don't have to click the Menu button in order to search for a particular drink; if you start to enter any name, the app assumes you want to search and takes it from there.

You can create a list of your favorite drinks and you can add your own recipes if you've invented or adapted a drink, or if you somehow come across one that is not included in the huge database that is part of the package. And this is a fully mobile application — no Internet or other connection required.

So I put it to the test. I wanted to know the proper recipe for a Sidecar, a very old-fashioned mixed drink that dates back to the early 1900s, a time when I'm pretty sure they did not have BlackBerry apps. The Sidecar was supposedly first served at the famed Ritz Hotel in Paris. It may have been a favorite of a man who arrived at the bar in a motorcycle sidecar, which is one way to bring a designated driver. I punched in the name, and there was the recipe: cognac, Curaçao liqueur, and fresh lemon juice. Excuse me while I take a break for lunch and a Sidecar.

Best features

The app shows the signs of polishing by pros; it is intuitive and smooth, which may or may not be your condition after you've tried it out at a bar.

Worst features

Please, don't drink and drive.

The app occupies about 3.2MB of device memory. You can run up quite a bar tab if you work your way through the 12,000 or so recipes. . . and think twice about drinking and calling all the names in your BlackBerry's contact list. Finally, take care not to drop your BlackBerry in your drink; I'm pretty sure that will void your warranty.

How to get it

Available from third-party sites such as Crackberry and the developer. Adorno. www.adornoapp.com. Price: $3.99–$7.99.

Fast Food Calorie Counter
$ US

You want fries with that? Wait: Do you want to eat anything at all at Kentucky Pizza McBurger Queen? If you're not already on a diet, you just might start one after you've spent a little time using the Fast Food Calorie Counter on your BlackBerry. This slim little app includes more than 5,900 menu items from 55 popular fast food chains. That's pretty impressive, and so are the numbers it spews out when you consult it; I'd suggest doing so on an empty stomach.

First, let's set a reference point. The federal Food and Drug Administration puts forth its Recommended Daily Allowances for things like calories, fat, sodium, and cholesterol. Just like pants, one size does not fit all. But the general range for an average person is sup-posed to be something like this:

- ✔ About 2,000 total calories per day
- ✔ No more than 65 grams of total fat, of which saturated fat should account for 20 grams or less
- ✔ Total sodium of about 2,300 mg
- ✔ Total cholesterol of no more than 300 grams

In general, the numbers should be a bit less for most women and cer-tainly less for people with any kind of underlying medical condition (including obesity).

And so, let us consult the menus in this app.

- ✔ If you are a visitor to Burger King, consider this order: a triple Whopper with cheese, a large package of French fries, and a large chocolate milk shake. It totals 2,580 calories all by itself, with

131 grams of total fat. In other words, if you eat just that meal you're over your limit for the full day and halfway into the next.

✔ I'm not just picking on the King. If you start your day with a Deluxe Breakfast with Syrup at McDonald's, you're more than halfway through your caloric recommendation and through with fat for the day: 1,320 calories and 59 grams of fat.

✔ And pizza: almost anywhere you go, figure on 300 to 350 calories and 16 grams of fat per slice before you add pepperoni, sausage, and extra cheese.

But its biggest shortcoming is that it is merely a listing. Not that I go to any of these fast-fooderies, but if I did I'd like to be able to input the exact order I am considering and see the potential total damage I may be about to inflict. Instead, I have to look at items one at a time and do my own accounting, which just might make the fellow in line behind me start grumbling.

That said, the most difficult thing about this app may be getting the grease marks off the screen of the BlackBerry.

Best features

It can't hurt to consult this app regularly. Substituting a salad (with a low-calorie non-fat dressing) for deep-fried grease just might save your life.

Worst features

You should be able to enter a list of the food you propose to eat and get a totalized report. I also wonder why the makers did not include sodium in their listings of foods; medical research has shown that excessive salt may be even more dangerous than too much sugar for some people.

How to get it

Available from third-party sites such as Crackberry and the developer. Mobigloo. www.mobigloo.com. Price: $4.99.

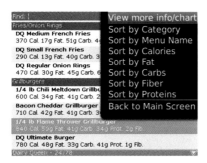

iSpyCams for BlackBerry
$ US

Dick Tracy had his wrist radio. Maxwell Smart his shoe phone. And now the BlackBerry has iSpyCams. This is a form of guilt-free voyeurism or, if you prefer, a way to travel the world without leaving your chair. iSpyCams links your BlackBerry to hundreds of public webcams around the world. You can choose by country or city, by location (beaches, cafés, and hotels are always in demand), what's most popular with other viewers these days.

The public cameras available in this app include those set up by tourist bureaus, hotels, attractions, sporting arenas, and parks. Some present still images refreshed every minute or so, while a handful are live video.

Across a few minutes I checked out the Eiffel Tower in Paris at sunset, jumped across the English Channel to the Abbey Road webcam to watch a bunch of tourists re-creating the cover of the 1969 Beatles album named after that crosswalk, flew across the Atlantic to Saint John in New Brunswick to check the harbor conditions, and finished up with a glimpse at a beach in Maui.

At many of the sites you are able to examine a "camera card" that tells you a bit more about the location being shown. And some of the cards link to a Web site with even more details. As I said, this is low-level voyeurism. Even though the quality of the images on the small screen of the BlackBerry is quite good, there is nothing in the standard set of camera locations that would outrage anyone's dignity.

It is educational, though, to realize that there are fewer and fewer public places we can travel to where we are completely out of view of a stranger on the Internet.

And then we go one step further: you can add your own webcam to the list. With a click of the tracking device on your BlackBerry you can look in on your own home. It depends on how you set it up: check in on the babysitter's handling of the kids, watch the front door for intruders, or arrange to have the family gather in front of the webcam while you are thousands of miles away on a business trip.

The standard setup for adding your own camera is to provide its Internet address and any password you have assigned. This would make it accessible on your BlackBerry only, unless you post a link for the world to see. If you do that, your webcam is no longer private but instead a public spot in cyberspace. And a word of warning: this app will eat up large amounts of data when used. Be careful if you do not have an unlimited data plan or if you are roaming away from home.

Best features

An amazing demonstration of the power and reach of the Internet and the ability of the BlackBerry to tap into it.

Worst features

Where are the models? The people on the beaches I visited would benefit from more formal attire. Seriously, the only issue is that some of the webcams take a few seconds to a minute to load their images the first time they are visited each session. That's not a high price to pay when you consider all of the technological leaps that are being crossed to bring an image to your BlackBerry.

How to get it

Available from third-party sites such as Crackberry and the developer. SKJM. www.skjm.com. Price: $2.99.

Links Scorecard
$ US

I understand the appeal of golf: it's a pleasant diversion from the hustle and bustle of everyday life, a chance to get out into a prettified version of the country, and an opportunity to relax with friends, family, and business acquaintances without any stress. That's the theory, at least. Speaking for myself, I think golf is a maddening public demonstration of my athletic shortcomings. And I fear for the safety of any person or any electronic device that is within 100 yards (on a really good day) of where I am standing with club in hand.

That said, there are going to be some golfers out there who will really like Links Scorecard, a BlackBerry app that takes away one of the stresses of the game: keeping score. Note that I say it will help with scoring; it is not going to reduce the number of strokes you take.

This is a nicely designed individual scorecard for golf. You can set up the scorecard before you leave for a day's game or do it as you slowly progress out and back on the course. To enter scores, select Play from the main menu and choose from a course you have already entered into the app. Or you can create a card on the spot which may or may not be annoying to others in your foursome and those waiting to tee off behind you.

Pebble Beach

Hole	2	3	4	5	6	7	8	9	10	Total
Par	4	4	4	3	5	3	4	4	4	39
Dist	502	374	327	187	500	106	416	462	430	3680
Score	7	5	6	4	10	①	8	7	6	60

CONCRETE
((:SOFTWARE

As you play each hole, you can stop to enter data about how you're doing. Did the ball go straight down the fairway or did it hook or slice to the left or right? How many yards did your first drive travel off the tee? Did the ball land on the green? (Hah!) Or in the sand? Did you record a sand save to get back to the green? (Really?) How about any up-and-downs from the green?

And then you enter the number of strokes (and penalties) and stand back to admire your score card. Right there, for all the world to see, are your eagles (two strokes below par on a hole), birdies (one stroke below par), and bogies (one above) highlighted with colorful symbols. You can look at the stats for any game in progress and for as many as you would like to hold on to for posterity. (Some you may want to delete immediately and never, ever discuss again.)

I suppose someone out there might be really interested in knowing the percentage of times a drive off the tee went right or left of the fairway or the percentage of times a ball hit the green in the regulation number of strokes. I mean, it couldn't hurt, right?

Why I even notated a beautiful hole-in-one, an ace, on the seventh hole at Pebble Beach. You can see it in the picture with this review, circled in red by the app. It's a bald-faced lie, of course, but a nice demonstration of what is possible. For someone else.

Best features

It won't make your game any worse.

Worst features

It is not easy to keep track of multiple players at the same time. And it would also be nice if there was a way to download information about major courses rather than having to enter par and distance manually.

How to get it

Available from BlackBerry App World and from third-party sites such as Crackberry. Concrete Software. www.concretesoftware.com. Price: $4.99.

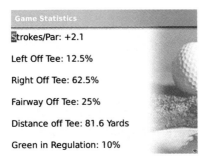

Game Statistics

Strokes/Par: +2.1

Left Off Tee: 12.5%

Right Off Tee: 62.5%

Fairway Off Tee: 25%

Distance off Tee: 81.6 Yards

Green in Regulation: 10%

Nobex Radio Companion
Free

We've come a long, long way from the days when a radio could pick up a dozen or so local stations. On a good day, with a big antenna. First the radios got smaller and smaller. Then they became portable. More recently came the Internet which took their signal out of the air and onto the World Wide Web. Oh, and now we have smartphones like the BlackBerry that can connect to the Internet.

You can see where this has taken us, right? Nobex Radio Companion uses your BlackBerry to connect to the Web and from there tap into any of a stream of perhaps 5,000 radio stations from more than 80 countries around the world. A moment to consider the technology here, please: A digital recording of music is played at a station, converted to a signal that is put out onto the Internet, then on request from your phone, it is broadcast as a radio signal that is picked up by your BlackBerry and played wherever you are. An alternate route is to use the Wi-Fi receiver in advanced BlackBerry models to communicate with the Internet without using the cellphone datastream.

In some ways, this is the future of "narrowcasting" we were all told to expect. In preparing this review I sat at my desk on a small island in Massachusetts and requested, then listened to, stations in Chicago, Los Angeles, London, Rome, and Sophia in Bulgaria. And Nobex goes a few steps beyond for some of the stations in the United States. There you can see a playlist of current and recent songs, request more information about the artist or the album, purchase a track, and even — for certain songs — ask to see the lyrics.

The app comes with a few sample stations, but the real power comes when you choose to add your own spectrum of sound. You can look at the entire list, or you can ask for a display by genre: rock, country, talk radio, oldies, and many other categories. You can also consult Nobex's Web site on a computer to see a map of available stations.

Once you select a station, it takes anywhere from a few seconds to a few minutes for Nobex to locate the Internet stream, direct it to your phone, and buffer some of the signal in your BlackBerry device's memory. The use of the buffer avoids some but not all dropouts of the signal that occur on the long and winding road back to the source.

I did find that some stations were more likely to deliver smooth and uninterrupted music while others would go away for seconds at a time; there's not anything you can do except hope for better conditions another time or hope that the transmitting radio station improves their equipment.

The app is available in two versions: a free edition that includes some audio advertisements and is limited to stations in your home country, and a worldwide subscription edition that allows you to skip the ads and offers some other advanced features. The subscription version was priced at $3.99 per month as this book went to press.

Best features

This is another one of those "gee whiz" apps to show someone who doesn't understand the power of a smartphone. And it would be even more impressive to use Nobex Radio Companion with something like the Jabra Cruiser speakerphone which connects to your BlackBerry by Bluetooth and can play music through its own speakers or retransmit the station to the FM radio in your car or your home or office.

Worst features

If you don't have an unlimited data plan or are roaming away from home, think twice or thrice or more before using Nobex over the cell-phone signal; it's going to run up quite a bill. If you're equipped to use Wi-Fi at your location, that should bring the data charges down to zero.

How to get it

Available from BlackBerry App World and from third-party sites such as Crackberry. Nobex Technologies Inc. www.nobexrc.com. Price: Free for your country; $3.99–$49.99 for more subscriptions.

Sid Meier's Railroad Tycoon
$ US

Now this is a serious waste of time. And for some BlackBerry users, that's a good thing. In fact, this is the sort of game you might just get away with claiming as an educational tool.

Sid Meier is one of the pioneers of personal computer games, specifically the genre of simulations. Meier's signature game was Civilization which was released in 1991; Railroad Tycoon preceded it by a year. Across two decades of amazing developments in graphics and sound and other bells and whistles, both of those early games have stood the test of time; as I said, they're serious.

The arrival of Railroad Tycoon on the BlackBerry brings both good and bad news. It's basically the same intriguing mental exercise that first captured the minds of millions of personal computer gamers, except that it is greatly squeezed down to fit on the small screen of your phone. Obviously compromises had to be made, but the small display does have the advantage of focusing your eyes and mind on the task at hand. There's not enough room for much distraction.

Think of yourself as one of the great railroad builders in the days before highways, environmental protection laws, and hardly anything else in the way of regulation. It was a time of pure capitalism: can you build a railroad from a source of product or passengers and deliver it to a market or a factory or an immigrant city? And most importantly, can you make a profit?

That's the underlying question of Railroad Tycoon. This is not an outerspace shoot-em-up or a version of football or baseball or tennis. It's that other sport — the one that obsessed America and other parts of the world in the late 19th century.

You begin with a bit of investment capital and a map of the wide-open spaces. You can research supply and demand and choose locations to connect. Then you investigate the relative costs of various routes; a straight line with bridges over rivers and tunnels through mountains is going to be much faster and potentially generate more income, but it will cost considerably more to build than a line that avoids obstacles. And if you need to, you can borrow money by selling bonds. You build track, stations, bridges, or tunnels if you must. You manage your finances, balancing debt against potential profit.

In the end, you win by producing a balance sheet that shows a profit. You lose by building a railroad to nowhere, or an expensive line that loses money. As you advance through the game — I mean, the simulation — you will be able to take on more difficult challenges. All of the interaction takes place with the use of the trackpad or trackball on your BlackBerry or selection from menus.

Meier was not directly involved in the conversion of his original game to run on the BlackBerry; in fact, the original PC version of the game is now available as a free download. Search the Internet to find one. But the version on the BlackBerry can come with you on the subway or Amtrak (perhaps you can come up with a new business plan for that benighted operation), and that's pretty impressive.

Best features

This little game exercises the muscle between your ears. There is a reason it has been popular for more than 20 years.

Worst features

Navigation on the screen using a trackpad in a current model BlackBerry is a bit mushy. Overall, it's a slow-paced game.

How to get it

Available from BlackBerry App World and from third-party sites such as Crackberry. Concrete Software. www.concretesoftware.com. Price: $4.99.

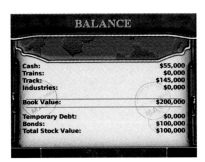

Aces Solitaire Pack 2
$ US

I've seen smart people, not-smart people, rich people, working stiffs, propeller-head geeks, and people who claim to be unable to work a television remote control drop everything to play a game of solitaire on a computer. There's something addictive about the basic game (also called Klondike), and there's something maniacal about some of the advanced forms of the games: Spider, FreeCell, Pairing, Higher/Lower, Forty Thieves, and some of the odd variations like Clocks and Shamrocks.

If you're one of the afflicted, then Aces Solitaire Pack 2 will feed your obsession. This app includes no fewer than 40 styles of the game and a full set of bells and whistles including sound effects, stat tracking, and the chance to post your scores on the Internet so you can see how you stack up against the universe of time-wasters playing one of the games on a subway train, in one of the non-driving seats of a car, or in the back row of a college lecture hall. The games are ranked by difficulty and you can choose settings for each. If you need a Mulligan you can undo or redo a move.

It's a large app, occupying about 5MB of precious space in device memory. Only two nits to pick: the screen image is a bit small on some BlackBerry models and the response to the trackpad on current models is a bit mushy. Oh, and a third complaint: it's keeping me away from writing the rest of this book.

How to get it

Available from BlackBerry App World and third-party sites such as Crackberry. Concrete Software. www.concretesoftware.com. Price: $4.99.

Aces Traffic Pack
$ US

This app is a traffic hazard. It steals your time, diverts your attention, and otherwise occupies your mind.

Aces Traffic presents you with a puzzle. Your car is blocked by a whole bunch of inconsiderate, clueless, and incompetent drivers — in other words, your daily commute. Your assignment is to get it from its parking space to the exit as efficiently as possible, moving the other cars out of the way to clear a path. It's a whole lot harder than it sounds. Cars can only be moved in a straight line, backwards, or forwards. There are sedans, trucks, and even stretch limos in the way. And as you advance in levels there are potholes and barriers that obstruct some of the lanes.

The package comes with six levels of increasing difficulty, each with about 80 puzzles: that's about 480 ways to drive you mad. The game is very nicely designed with attractive colors and an appropriately annoying set of video game beeps and boops. It's a whole lot of fun. But please don't use it while driving.

How to get it

Available from BlackBerry App World and third-party sites such as Crackberry. Concrete Software. www.concretesoftware.com. Price: $4.99.

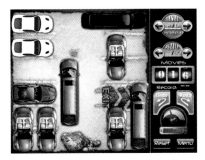

Flixster
Free

What we've got here is a BlackBerry version of the movie listings. You can choose a movie and find out where it's playing, or you can ask to see what's playing at theaters near you. There's just about every bell and whistle a movie lover could want: descriptions of new films, video trailers, photos, a cast list, and a listing of theaters.

Unlike a newspaper listing, you can ask this app to figure out where you are by using the GPS that is part of most current BlackBerry devices. Or you can enter a city and state or a Zip code to instruct it where to look. When you see the listings of movie theaters, they includes the phone number and a listing of the current slate of films now being shown, along with the time schedule.

You can check out which films are box-office hits and you can read brief snippets of reviews by professional critics or venture into the amateur world of social networking and find out what your fellow Flixster viewers think. Sometimes the critics and the patrons are in agreement, and sometimes there's a wide gulf between them. Then again, not every moviegoer is a 16-year-old.

The major downsides to this app are these: you have to look elsewhere to read full-length reviews of films, and the download of listings and especially of movie trailers can be quite slow.

How to get it

Available from BlackBerry App World and the developer. Flixster. www.flixster.com/mobile/apps/blackberry. Price: Free.

Greeting Cards Maker
$ US

Straight from the heart — and from your BlackBerry: birthday cards, expressions of love, wedding and baby congratulations, and other messages. The app on your BlackBerry is a small engine.

Most or all of the images and backgrounds exist on the server of the app maker Softbox; make sure you understand your cellphone's data plan.

And you can also use any photo that exists on your phone — images you have snapped using its built-in camera or downloaded to the phone from your computer or another device. You can add standard wishes in English, French, German, or Spanish, or enter your own words and even an emoticon if that's the sort of way you speak or write.

This app is simple and easy to use and makes no attempt at anything really strenuous like audio or video: just a picture or drawing, adorned with a short greeting from you. You can adjust the font, its size and color, and its position on the card.

And then you click E-mail and zap it to the one you love or the one you want to congratulate. E-mail only, not SMS text, and you should call your mother on the phone every once in a while, don't you think?

How to get it

Available through third-party sources such as Crackberry or directly from the manufacturer at http://www.softbox.com. Price: $1.99.

Moviefone
Free

This is the updated version of one of the first technological marvels to impact moviegoers: you could dial a phone number and enter a Zip code to get movie listings near you. We're talking more than 20 years ago, including an entire episode of "Seinfeld" that explored what happened when Kramer got a new phone number (for his telephone that was connected by a cord to the wall — can you imagine?) that was very close to the popular number for the service.

Moviefone has gone corporate, now a service of AOL. In the BlackBerry version, we have the basic elements: movie listings, trailers, and showtimes at theaters near a Zip code you enter. You can also see the movie's poster. One feature it offers not matched by many other services: the ability to order and pay for tickets online at some participating theaters.

What we don't have are reviews of the films other than an unexplained five-star rating; presumably this is based on an average of some group of opinions. And the app does not use the GPS in the BlackBerry, although it's not a huge issue to enter a Zip code. However, it only seems to show theaters within a few miles of that point. And like Flixster, its display of movie trailers is handcuffed by the speed of connection offered by your cellphone provider. In some places it may be quite good; at my office the trailers took a while to load and stopped often to catch their breath or their data.

How to get it

Available from BlackBerry App World and the developer. Moviefone. Price: Free.

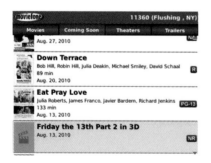

Next Dual Pack
$ US

Next! Another complete waste of time — a game that exercises the muscle between your ears, gets your mind off the day's trials and tribulations, and is oh-so-satisfying when you complete a particularly troublesome puzzle. Again, the BlackBerry is exceptional in its devotion to the real needs of people who need to accomplish real tasks. The beauty of an intelligent game like this one is that it helps you regain a bit of mental rigor: don't play around at a staff meeting or when the boss is waiting for you to finish that essential report. But at lunch, or on break time, a few carefully chosen minutes of mental exercise may be the best way to sweep aside the cobwebs that sometimes develop between your ears.

It began as Next, and was later improved and augmented and given the not-very-memorable name of Next Dual Pack. So now there are two levels of 64 puzzles each, a dual pack of dumbfounding puzzles. This game was written by the same cruel mind that developed Nintaii, which may either greatly impress or severely depress you. It's a deceptively simple challenge that starts out very easy but quickly becomes very complex and progresses to nearly (but apparently not impossibly) unfinishable.

The rules are so simple: remove all the blocks from the screen by joining same-colored blocks in groups of two or more. You'll get the hang of it pretty quickly, at least on the early puzzles; the later ones can hook you for hours.

How to get it
Available from BlackBerry App World and from third-party sites such as Crackberry. Mobigloo. www.mobigloo.com. Price: $4.99.

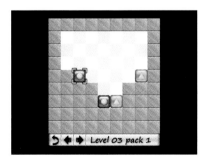

Nintaii
$ US

Nintaii is a Japanese word that roughly translates as "patience." You will need a great deal of nintaii to get through this deceptively simple game which mixes bits and pieces of checkers and pocket puzzles. The goal of the game is to get the block to fall into the exit hole at the end of each stage. You click the block and roll it forward or backward. So far, so good, except that the block is rectangular (two cells wide or tall) and the hole is square (one cell). And there are dead ends and roadblocks, and in later levels, switches that have to be activated by standing the block on them.

Nintaii. You'll get there eventually. There are 100 levels standing between your first attempt and the Zen-like happiness that can only come from fulfillment of a seemingly impossible task.

The game is very attractively designed and the trackball or trackpad on your BlackBerry handles the movement of the block very smoothly. I'm not going to claim to have completed this puzzle yet; I do have a book I need to finish writing. But I'll be back.

How to get it

Available from BlackBerry App World and from third-party sites such as Crackberry. Mobigloo. www.mobigloo.com. Price: $4.99.

Pinball Deluxe
$ US

A not small amount of my wasted youth was spent hanging around the candy store and waiting my turn to throw what little change I had into the slot of the pinball machine. These were true works of art: a wooden frame, hand-painted backlit glass screen, mechanical flippers, and wire frame chutes and alleys. Today some wealthy Internet tycoons have some of those very machines down in the basement rec room. Me, I've just added Pinball Deluxe to my BlackBerry, and to my surprise it's almost as much fun.

In any case, it's also a technological wonder. Pinball Deluxe is a beautiful little version of the game, complete with some of the smoothest and detailed graphics you're going to find on any handheld smartphone. And for me, the best part is the vibration you feel in the palm of your hand each time the ball strikes one of the bumpers. It wouldn't be the same without that.

There's not much to learn: push and hold the spacebar to retract the plunger and then let it go. Then watch the ball as it careens around the screen and wait for the optimum moment to let loose one of the flippers. The designers let you press any key on the left side for the left flipper and any on the right for the other. But after all these years, I was pleased to find that I still had the touch: I'm a pinball wizard once more.

How to get it
Available from BlackBerry App World and from third-party sites such as Crackberry. Mobigloo. www.mobigloo.com. Price: $4.99.

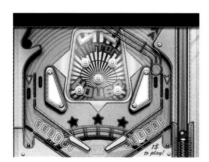

Round of Applause
$ US

Let's be honest. We all can use an occasional pat on the back, a heart-felt thank you, and a thunderous round of applause. It makes us feel appreciated, wanted, valuable. Sort of the same way you feel about your BlackBerry, right? But sometimes you can't always get what you want. That is, until the pranksters at Blackfox Innovations solved the problem.

Download Round of Applause to your BlackBerry, and with a click of a button you can let loose a polite smattering of claps, a rousing ovation, or even a cacophony of cheers and huzzahs. You can play them for yourself, or you can let loose the cheers for your boss or significant other. I'm planning on having one cued up to play at the end of the next lecture I give.

This simple application comes equipped with 20 variations of the round of applause. My only quibble: they are identified only as numbers when they could instead have been given names. (Standing Ovation with two Bravos!, for example.) But I go through my day much more self-assured knowing I can summon the cheers with a click.

How to get it

Available from BlackBerry App World and from third-party sites such as Crackberry. BlackFox Innovations. http://blackfoxinnovations.com. Price: $3.99.

Vorino Fractal Explorer
$ US

Far out. This is one of the most useless apps ever conceived for the BlackBerry. Some of us, though, cannot imagine life without a personal handheld fractal generator. It brings me right back to what I remember of my psychedelic days, only I'm clear-eyed and wide awake and completely unaffected by any pharmaceuticals. I do have the Jefferson Airplane playing "White Rabbit" on the office stereo system, though.

What's a fractal, you say? It's a mathematically calculated pattern using colors and geometric forms. A fractal can be split into parts, each of which is close to a reduced-size copy of the whole; that's called "self-similarity" and in the world of propeller heads that counts almost as much as having a girlfriend or boyfriend.

What's the use? Not much, except they're hypnotically pretty. You can stare at one for a while to productively waste time, and using this app you can save your favorites to the BlackBerry media card and use them as a wallpaper for your home screen.

There's not a whole bunch for you to do as owner of this app. You can choose the starting color and make some basic adjustments for the complexity of the drawing. And you can zoom into areas of the Mandelbrot fractal (named after mathematician Benoît Mandelbrot in 1975 and was derived from the Latin fractus meaning "broken" or "fractured"). And you can switch to the Julia set, which is a secondary dimension within the Mandelbrot.

How to get it
Available from BlackBerry App World and from third-party sites such as Crackberry. Vorino Software. www.vorino.com. Price: $2.99.

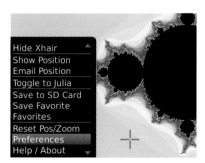

9 Ten Things That Make Your BlackBerry More Brilliant

Top Ten Accessories

- Memory
- Bluetooth headset
- Speakerphone
- Car clamps and hangers
- BlackBerry Presenter
- Spare cable

- Screen protection
- Power at home, in the car, and in an emergency
- CompanionLink Express
- Back-to-the-Future Desk Phone

Memory
$$ US

Let us give thanks for the memory in our BlackBerry devices. It is the presence of this form of electronic storage that allows our smartphone to keep track of contacts, calendar items, ringtones, pictures, videos, and settings we have made to personalize it. And it is also the memory that is used by the computer within our device to hold and run the small programs: the apps that we celebrate in this book.

Depending on how you intend to use your BlackBerry, the more memory, the merrier. That said, older models of the smartphone and older versions of its operating system have much lower maximums. Memory on a smartphone is very much like the memory on a personal computer, with one big difference: On a PC or a Macintosh or other computer, the memory (sometimes called RAM, or random access memory) is generally "non-persistent." What that means is that it requires a continual feed of electrical power so that it holds on to the information within tiny chips.

On a computer, to hold information permanently, the data is stored with magnetic markings on a hard disk drive or with optical markings on a CD or DVD disc. But on a smartphone (and on similarly ubiquitous digital cameras) the type of memory that is used is called flash memory. This technology accepts data when it is written there by the device and then holds on to it even when the power is turned off.

Now for the specifics of the BlackBerry device. All current models have two different types of flash memory:

- ✔ **Device memory** (also known as application or onboard memory). As the names suggest, this block of memory is built into the phone and is intended to hold apps as well as other essential elements, including the operating system. You cannot change the amount of device memory in your phone, but you can manage its use as best you can.

- ✔ **Media card** (sometimes called expansion or removable memory). This card is held inside your phone — either in a slot along one of its sides or (in some newer models) in a hideaway under the battery.

All named BlackBerry devices (including the Bold, Curve, Pearl, Storm, and Torch) as well as the unnamed BlackBerry 8800 are all capable of having and using a micro-SD media card. The older models, using Operating System 4.2.0 can work with a card as large as 2GB. The newer models, using OS 4.6 and later (including OS 5.0 and OS 6.0) can be used with a media card as big as 32GB in capacity.

All apps must reside in device memory. That's just the way BlackBerry has designed its phones. So to allow yourself the most space for personal items likes photos, music, and files, you should store these on the media card.

Depending on the phone you own and sometimes the cellphone carrier you purchased it from, your BlackBerry may have come with a media card or you may have had to purchase one separately. To find out the size of the card in your phone, press the Memory button and go down this path: Menu ➪ Settings ➪ Options ➪ Memory.

Photo courtesy of Sandisk Corporation

Some phones may have a slightly different route to the Options screen. You can always turn off your phone and open the hatch to remove the media card and look at its label. Or, call your cellphone provider for assistance.

As I said, the amount of media card memory you want will depend upon your needs. You'll want more if you intend to take a lot of photos or videos and store them on your phone or use your BlackBerry as a music player. I use my BlackBerry as an extra backup device for my critical computer files while I travel. I usually carry at least 1GB of files relating to lectures I present on the road — PowerPoint files, lecture notes, videos, and music. They are there if my laptop fails or goes missing, and I can also rehearse my presentations in the car (passenger seats only), on a plane, or even just before I go up on stage.

You can purchase a micro-SD media card from your cellphone provider or from an electronics store or online site. The cards come in varying sizes, and also are marked with their class. The class is a speed rating; the higher the class, the faster the card should be in storing or playing back data. Class 6 is better than Class 4, and so on.

Which brand to use? All of the major companies produce a good product: Kingston, Lexar, SanDisk, and Sony among them. If you see a brand you haven't heard of, fire up your BlackBerry and visit the Web to do a little research. There are a handful of smaller off-brand companies that might not be selling product worth your investment.

Check with your provider if you have any questions about the size and type your phone can use.

Prices for micro-SD cards range from about $10 for a 2GB to about $40 for a 32GB unit.

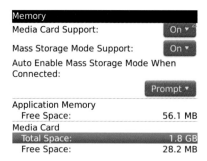

Bluetooth Headset
Jabra EXTREME: $130 US

As the full name explains, this is a headset — actually a single-ear set — that communicates with your BlackBerry using Bluetooth radio. And the "EXTREME" comes from Jabra's claim to eliminate background noise by as much as 24dB; it does this through digital signal processing that concentrates on the frequency of human voices and then also performs some other tricks to remove or reduce the volume of sound more distant than the mouth nearest to the earphone. As with other Jabra devices it uses a pair of microphones that the circuitry can sample to make adjustments as necessary.

There's also an automatic volume control which adjusts to the environment. The included car charger also serves as a storage stand for the headset; there's also an AC charger.

The fact is that not all headsets fit well on all people. Jabra EXTREME is one of the more universal devices I have seen, equipped with your choice of large or small ear hooks. The headset weighs 10 grams (about a third of an ounce). The battery is said to offer 5.5 hours of talk time and as much as 10.5 days of standby time.

You answer a call by tapping the central button on the earpiece; press the button a second time to end the call. That's fully within the law, officer.

Available from online retailers including Amazon. www.jabra.com.

Photo courtesy of Jabra

Speakerphone
Jabra CRUISER: $50 US

The built-in speakerphone on a BlackBerry is just barely acceptable; that's where the Jabra CRUISER comes in. It uses several advanced technologies to improve both ends of the conversation: dual microphones and special digital signal processing circuitry take away much of the noise around you and audio enhancements improve the sound that comes from its much larger speaker.

But it doesn't stop there. You can instruct the CRUISER to rebroadcast the incoming side of the phone call so that it plays on the FM radio in your car or your office. And when you're not using the phone, the same FM transmitter can send music stored on your BlackBerry to a channel on your stereo system.

The Jabra CRUISER communicates with your BlackBerry using Bluetooth radio, which eliminates the need for wires. In a car, it can clip to the sun visor so that it is out of the way but in a good location to talk to you and listen to your responses. You tap a button to answer or end a call. Other buttons turn on the FM transmitter and play or pause music

With most current BlackBerry models, the device will automatically pair to your phone, and it can also access your contacts folder so that it can announce the name of any incoming caller for whom it finds a match. The unit's rechargeable battery is rated for as many as 10 hours of talk or rebroadcast time and as many as 13 days on standby; a car charger is included. The unit itself is about the same size as a BlackBerry device.

Available from online retailers including Amazon. www.jabra.com.

Photo courtesy of Jabra

Car Clamps and Hangers

Arkon Travelmount BB215: $20 US
Arkon SM514 Slim-Grip Universal Phone Holder: $20 US
Arkon SM512 Friction Dashboard Mount: $20 US
Arkon Sports Armband for Smartphones: $15

When most of us need to hold a BlackBerry to our ear, we can give it a hand. That doesn't work well, though, when you're driving. I've already written about the advantages of using a headset or a speakerphone in the car. With the latest versions of smartphones, we've moved even further down the road. Current BlackBerry devices include GPS circuitry that can give you on-screen directions and audio instructions to your destination. You also can use your devices to play back music or to announce and read incoming e-mail.

The need here is for a mechanism to hold our phones for us in the car. It's not as simple as it might seem: BlackBerry devices come in many different shapes, and no two models of vehicle are exactly the same when it comes to places to mount a holder. And there are safety concerns as well: mounts can't block airbags or obstruct the view out the window or be placed in such a way that they can become unexpected dangers in an accident.

Photo courtesy of Arkon Resources, Inc.

There are many manufacturers of BlackBerry accessories for the car; I've picked one of them because I find their products to be well designed and because they seem to have a solution for problems most of us haven't even realized we have.

✔ The **Arkon Travelmount BB215** holds BlackBerry Curve, Tour, and Bold (models 9650 and 9700) devices. It can mount to the windshield, dashboard, or the console; a mini suction cup grabs hold of the glass directly or you can attach an adhesive-backed mounting disc elsewhere and have it glom onto that.

✔ Arkon also offers a line of holders that aren't specific to a particular phone. The **Arkon SM514 Slim-Grip Universal Phone Holder** can be used with a wide range of BlackBerry phones and even devices from other companies if you must. The holder is spring-loaded at the bottom: push the grip down with the bottom of your phone until it is safely held and then release to clamp it in place. It, too, can attach to the windshield, dashboard, or console.

✔ The **Arkon SM512 Friction Dashboard Mount** is a universal phone holder that adds a small weighted dashboard mount (also known as a beanbag holder). The mount has a non-slip bottom and enough weight to hold on to the phone in most situations. I use a beanbag to hold the GPS unit in my car and find it generally works well; the advantage to me is that I can easily take the whole apparatus with me when I travel and install it in a rental car without making any permanent alterations. Each of the Arkon holders I've mentioned is available from major retailers and online stores.

✔ There's one other device worth mentioning for some of you: the **Arkon Sports Armband for Smartphones.** It attaches to your upper arm with an adjustable Velcro strap and holds your smartphone at close hand as you jog through the streets of New York or compete in the Boston Marathon. It's sweat resistant, and it even includes reflective markers so that the cars coming up on you at night can see you better. (Let's hope they're not on the phone and distracted.)

Photo courtesy of Arkon Resources, Inc.

BlackBerry Presenter

BlackBerry Presenter: $200 US

You have a tiny computer with a fairly substantial block of memory. And in that memory you have your business plan laid out in a PowerPoint presentation, a set of Excel spreadsheets that show actual and potential cash flow and profits, and some gorgeous beauty shots of your products. And then you walk into the conference room and realize that you left your laptop in the taxi.

The BlackBerry Presenter, made and marketed by Research in Motion, adds video output (and some software conversion) to your BlackBerry. You plug one end into a video projector, just like a laptop. And then you connect it to your BlackBerry with a wireless Bluetooth radio link.

The Presenter automatically detects and takes advantage of the highest available resolution, from 640×480 (VGA) to 1024×768 (XGA). It outputs to a projector with a VGA or S-Video cable, and can work with either the NTSC signal (used in North America and some other nations) or PAL (used through most of Europe and elsewhere).

On the software side, the Presenter supports 24 animations and 55 transitions that are standard for PowerPoint. (The Documents To Go app reviewed in this book does not support animations and transitions and is mostly intended for use in editing or creating simple files that are transferred to a laptop or desktop computer for presentation.) It works with most current BlackBerry devices (except the BlackBerry Curve 8300 series and the BlackBerry Pearl Flip 8200 series). Check with RIM to make certain your model is supported.

Available from Research in Motion. www.BlackBerry.com/presenter.

Photo courtesy of Research in Motion

Spare Cable
Various vendors: $5 US

When the USB standard was introduced for use with computers, it was hailed as a one-design-fits-all solution. If only that were true: although USB has proven to be a very useful standard for interconnection of a mind-boggling array of devices, today there are no fewer than five officially recognized connector types. (There are also a few unofficial connectors, including one used in some devices by Apple Computer.)

In any case, current models of BlackBerry devices have a Micro USB port on the phone itself. That port can be connected to the AC adapter or a car charger to power up the battery or operate the phone when the battery does not have sufficient voltage. And the same port can be used to connect to a desktop or laptop computer to exchange files or to use the BlackBerry Desktop Manager software. To do that, you need a USB–Micro USB cable. One end has the standard USB connector and plugs into the computer; the other end attaches to the smartphone.

I always carry at least one extra USB–Micro USB cable in my kit to allow for data transfer and to permit me to recharge my phone from a computer. A no-name cable costs just a few dollars and is available from many online sites and retail stores. A BlackBerry brand cable may be priced higher; there is no reason a generic cable should not do the job.

Screen Protection
Trü Protection: $15 US

Some people keep their BlackBerry in mint condition, polishing its screen regularly and storing it in a suede-lined case when it is not carefully held in the hand. Others toss it in their pocket along with cookie crumbs and coins, or drop it to the bottom of a purse where it rattles around with all kinds of stuff.

If you're the polishing kind of person, I recommend using a screen film or screen protector. This is especially valuable if you have a BlackBerry model with a touch screen like the Tour or the Torch, but any smartphone can benefit from a quality film that minimizes glare, reduces fingerprints, and helps prevent scratches.

One such product is Trü Protection, which is precut to fit your particular model's display and is attached by static cling. A number of manufacturers offer similar products; make sure you get one that is as clear and thin as possible.

While I'm on the subject of taking care of your BlackBerry, let me review a pair of common ways your marvelous device can be magically transformed into an expensive paperweight:

- ✔ Gravity: Most BlackBerry devices are nicely balanced and they will also survive most short falls, but I recommend against dropping it from your hand onto the sidewalk; the concrete will win. Keep a tight grip on your device and use a protective case to cushion it when not in use.

- ✔ Water: Think twice about unholstering it in a rainstorm. Inside the phone, near the battery, is a little strip of paper that turns color if the phone gets wet; that's the first place your cellphone provider will look if you bring in a dead phone and ask for a warranty repair.

Available from Research in Motion, third-party resellers, and from the developer. Trü Protection. www.truprotection.com.

Power at Home, in the Car, and in an Emergency

Various sources: $5–$50 US

The rechargeable battery in your BlackBerry is a marvel. A tiny Lithium Ion battery in a BlackBerry can provide several days' use as a phone or a data device and can sit in standby mode — powered on and listening — for many more days. And it can be recharged.

But sooner or later, that battery is going to run out of juice. I recommend the following items for the road warrior:

- ✔ A car charger. This device plugs into what used to be called the cigarette lighter in vehicles but is now mostly referred to as the accessory outlet. It takes power from the vehicle and adjusts it to the proper level to recharge your phone; you can also use your BlackBerry while it is being charged. Expect to pay between $5 and $10.

- ✔ An extra AC charger. No matter how organized you are, sooner or later you are going to find yourself a stranger in a strange place without the charger that sits on your desk or at your bed- side at home. I keep a second charger in my laptop bag at all times and sometimes a third one in the suitcase I use most often. An AC charger should cost about $10.

- ✔ An extra battery. Although you can charge and recharge the battery of your BlackBerry hundreds of times, eventually it will lose its ability to accept a full charge or hold on to its power. A BlackBerry brand battery (your safest bet) should cost between $10 and $20.

KIWICHOICE

Emergency Power Source
Kiwi U-Powered KWS1: $50 US

I got a real charge out of this new accessory when it arrived on the market as I was writing this book: it combines a backup battery, an AC charger, a car charger, and a USB (computer output) charger, all of which should be enough to prove its worth. But it goes one step further: in a pinch (and on a bright sunny day) it can generate its own electricity.

The Kiwi U-Powered KWS1 includes its own lithium battery with a capacity of 2000 mAh (more juice than the typical BlackBerry battery holds) along with chargers that can top it off. It also includes a set of 11 different connector tips so that its battery can connect to just about any portable device: a BlackBerry, of course, but also nearly every other brand of smartphone, GPS, music player, digital camera, or what-have-you.

And then it goes green: if you are not near a car, an AC outlet, or a computer USB port you can still recharge the Kiwi. Open up it up like a fan to reveal three photovoltaic panels that can convert sunlight into voltage. Truth be told, using solar power is considerably slower than plugging into the wall outlet: it takes at least 17 hours of sun to fully charge the Kiwi's battery. But then again, you're burning no carbon. Three magnets on the back of the charger allow you to stick it to a metal surface.

List price for the unit is about $50 and it is available from retailers, online sources, and from the manufacturer. www.kiwichoice.com.

Photo courtesy of Kiwi Choice

CompanionLink Express
CompanionLink: $70 US

With current versions of the BlackBerry Desktop Manager, RIM has taken a baby step toward recognizing the persistence of the Palm Pilot: using the Device Switch Wizard, you can upload calendar and contact information from the Palm Desktop to your BlackBerry. But for reasons no one at RIM has been able to explain, the transfer is forward-looking only: calendar events from this moment into the future.

I stumbled across the solution all by myself: a nifty tool called CompanionLink Express. It's a piece of software that installs on your PC and can communicate with RIM's BlackBerry Desktop Manager.

You have only a few settings to make: choosing a calendar as the source, choosing a calendar as the target, and instructing the software how to handle deletions it finds at one end or the other.

You can try out CompanionLink Express free for 14 days and buy a copy of your own for $69.95. And there's also a Pro version that adds a few advanced options such as syncing to multiple phones and multiple databases; the Pro also allows you to subscribe to wireless sync using CompanionLink's secure servers for an additional $9.95 per month.

Available from the developer at www.companionlink.com.

Back-to-the-Future Desk Phone
Moshi Moshi 01: $30 US

This product just proves the axiom that everything old is new again. It also proves that Ma Bell had it just about right when they designed the first one-piece handsets for telephones: a dumbbell-shaped unit with a speaker at one end and a microphone at the other. It cradles easily between shoulder and neck. That's why I love the Moshi Moshi 01 handset from Native Union. It's a retro-style desktop handset (available in basic black or, if you must, hot red) that has a discreetly hidden plug that attaches to your BlackBerry's audio output. There's also a model that communicates using Bluetooth, although that requires an extra power connector.

The speaker and microphone in the Moshi Moshi device help reduce background noise. And you will be distancing yourself from any possible problems related to RF radiation emanating from your smartphone.

Moshi Moshi connects to your BlackBerry with an included cable that plugs into the standard audio headset jack. The cable is long enough that you can stash your BlackBerry out of sight. The desktop phone does not require a connection to an electrical source — it is powered by your smartphone. There is no dial on the phone (you still use your BlackBerry for that) but there is one little button on the handset: press it once to pick up a call and press it a second time to hang up.

Available from retailers and online sites as well as the manufacturer. www.nativeunion.com.

Photo courtesy of Native Union